THE RÉSUMÉ
OF LIFE

Becoming Consciously Aware through
Spirit, Mind, and Body

TERRY J. WALKER, MA

BALBOA.
PRESS

A DIVISION OF HAY HOUSE

Balboa Press books may be ordered through booksellers or by contacting:

Balboa Press
A Division of Hay House
1663 Liberty Drive
Bloomington, IN 47403
www.balboapress.com
1 (877) 407-4847

Print information available on the last page.

ISBN: 978-1-5043-9135-1 (sc)
ISBN: 978-1-5043-9137-5 (hc)
ISBN: 978-1-5043-9136-8 (e)

Library of Congress Control Number: 2017916788

Balboa Press rev. date: 11/27/2017

CONTENTS

In Loving Memory of Walter W. Dykes
(1903–1996)

To my Pappaw, who was the patriarch of our family and one of my greatest advocates. You played an important role in my life and my upbringing. You stood beside me when times were difficult. You taught me about spirituality and to be the best I could be. You also taught me that it is not important *who* you love—only *that* you love.

Although it took many years for me to try to understand, I finally got it and have come full circle. Although you are not here on the physical plane, I know you are with me every single day in spirit, and I know you are proud. I love you!

ACKNOWLEDGMENTS

THIS BOOK IS DEDICATED TO all those who have been in my life for a *reason* or a *season*. As I have learned, we are *all* connected. We are here and in each other's lives to learn, to teach, to experience, and to grow. The lessons I have encountered have been both joyful and difficult, but whatever the lesson or the experience and whatever the outcome, the path has led me to here and now!

I want to recognize and thank my wonderful mother and father because without you none of this would have been possible. You loved me and supported me through my journey. You may not have always agreed with my choices, but you were always there to encourage me, to strengthen me, and to love me. You believed in me and helped me to remain strong through the good times and not-so-good times. For all your support and love, words cannot express the love, gratitude, and respect I have for you. I thank you, I love you, and I am so grateful for all you've done for me. You have always stood beside me and loved me no matter what. This is a gift I will always cherish, and now you have allowed me to share my gift with others.

Thank you to my grandparents! I know you are with me in spirit every day. You encouraged me to fulfill my dreams! You always said it didn't matter what I did in life—just that I do it to the best of my ability, be kind to others, and always treat others as equals. Your love and inspiration have been the cornerstone of where our family is today.

To Stacy and Braxton: I have had the privilege of having a relationship that settled me down in so many ways, shared the joy of a son, and had the opportunity to watch him grow and become a spectacular young man, beaming with goodness and light that continues to grow and illuminate from him. Never lose your creativity and your love, as I am so very proud of you. Stacy, you always said I was meant to do more and I *needed to fly.* So here I go!

To my family, friends, colleagues, and clients who have supported me in so many ways: You know who you are, and you know I love you!

Your support was the encouragement that helped sustain me with some type of knowing that maybe I did have a positive impact and that I mattered. There were so many times I did not believe in myself, which held me in a great deal of struggle. Thank you for your encouragement, your friendship, your support, and your love. I had to finally realize that I am not alone, I am loved, and I have impacted others in a positive way. I now realize that is why we are here, and that was the starting line toward finding my purpose and how this book finally came to be.

To Shelli, Margie, Diana, and Tania, my ole high school buddies who have returned to my life after many years. You reminded me of who I was and who I am. (Notice I said *ole* and not *old*, as you also reminded me of the importance of staying young at heart.) After high school, we embarked on our separate journeys, and I am so very grateful our paths have come back together to allow a new and wiser journey. After our conversations, I realized you did not judge me and that you loved me for the person I was and for the person I have become. Thank you.

To Deb: We've traveled many miles together, and our friendship has spanned a few decades. You've helped to settle me down through many times of chasing after crazy ideas. You've always been my constant go-to friend. You've supported me through many of my internal and external struggles. I am so grateful you have been such a large part of my life. This time, you've allowed me to find myself, as you realized this was something I had to do on my own. Thank you, my dear friend!

I want to thank Jen and Nicole! You both entered my life at the right time for the right reasons. Once I surrendered and allowed myself to be open to accepting, trusting, listening, and learning, my life changed. When I finally realized I had done all I could do on my own, you entered my life. The two of you have been godsends. I am so grateful God brought you into my life. I guess the saying is true—"When the student is ready, the teacher will appear." You both catapulted me into a completely new way of living, thinking, and believing. Spirit, mind, and body are coming together to operate as a whole. Thank you!

To my good buddy Spring-er!: We have pounded the streets as colleagues and traveled many miles together. Somewhere in those travels, we became great friends. You believed in me when I couldn't believe in myself, and you once told me, "Terry, you just didn't know what you are capable of." That stuck with me, and now I believe I'm finding out! Thank you, my friend!

To my little Apeee: You are the little sister I never had! Thank you for coming into my life and being wise beyond your years. I don't know how you did it, but somehow you grew on me, and I'm so grateful to have the opportunity to watch you grow and blossom! You have a beautiful, strong, independent soul, and I am so glad that we are friends … sisters.

To Shea, my boss and my friend: You've been such a support and protector of me. No matter what we encountered, you were always there. Thanks for being the one I could call during those long, difficult days on the road and allowing me the opportunity to sing.

To Jim and Dottie: You've always been such a support to me, and I am so grateful to call you friends. To see the relationship you have and to know you are best friends to each other gives me hope that people can truly enjoy each other and share their journeys in joy and fun. What a special gift you have. Thank you!

To Mike and Vickie: Thank you for your friendship, love, and support. Vickie, I have always cherished our long talks, and please know you have been such a blessing in my life. You have always encouraged me to follow my dreams, and now I'm beginning to do just that! Thank you!

To Robin White, my long-lost friend and colleague: You made the effort to find me after many years, and I am so grateful that you did. Thank you for coming back into my life at the right time for the right reasons. You found me; you took my hand and helped motivate me to finish the book. On top of that, you introduced me to Dr. Massey. Thank you, my friend.

To Dr. Angela Massey, my editor and friend: Thank you for coming into my life at the right time for the right reasons. Again—"When the student is ready, the teacher will appear." Once I was ready but not quite sure what to do with the book, you and Robin appeared. You took me under your wing and helped me to strengthen the essence of the book. You helped to close the gaps and pushed me to bring it all together. You believed in the book, and you believed in me. I am so grateful to have you in my life. Thank you!

To Dr. Wayne Dyer, Ms. Louise Hay, Deepak Chopra, Marianne Williamson, Oprah Winfrey, and all the other new thought leaders of our time: You have helped to open my eyes to a new way of understanding, and I am so grateful. You've paved the way in opening hearts and minds. I can only hope and pray that I may join among your ranks in this positive, loving, new way of being.

And the greatest thank-you of all—thank you, God! I now know, and I now believe! This all came from you! I am so grateful to finally wake up to a new discovery and understanding. I have a whole new way of life, of living, of thinking, of seeing, and of believing! Thank you for setting off my alarm clock and for not letting me push the snooze button anymore. You have written this book through me, and I can only pray it will serve to awaken and inspire others.

FOREWORD

I AM TRYING TO REMEMBER when Terry and I first met and how we became such good friends. It just seems that we always were friends. I'm sure I was drawn to her constant smile and infectious laugh. Terry definitely has the *best* laugh ever! She ended up being the only reason that I made it through a horrible high school algebra class. (Mr. Sorrelli, so sorry for all the disruptions!)

Terry always had such a brightness about her. She is such a good, kind, and wise soul! After graduation, we entered adulthood and began our life journeys. I watched as Terry, like you, experienced some incredible moments of happiness and, like you, experienced some incredible moments of pain. The one that stands out to me as the most devastating *and* the most useful was the end of a long-term relationship. Terry was heartbroken. She had lost her family and her life as she knew it. I could tell that my friend wasn't sure how she could move forward and ever be truly happy again. Sadly, her brightness had dimmed. She began asking, "How did I find myself here? How will I ever move on?"

It was during this time that she began to climb out of the sadness and began her journey to heal herself—her spirit, mind, and body. It was a beautiful transformation—a journey that has made her strong and truly content with herself. She did this with God and the tools that she had always possessed, the tools we all possess!

After reading this book, I thought about the classic movie *The Wizard of Oz* and Judy Garland's character, Dorothy, and her ruby-red slippers. The slippers held magical powers that could help Dorothy get back home, yet Dorothy doesn't tap into their power until the end of the movie. Finally, she clicks her heels three times and says those five words that take her back to her beloved Kansas. It was much easier than Dorothy had imagined. She always had the power, but she didn't know how easy it was to use it.

Terry's thought-provoking words made me realize that we all have a power within. And in this book she answers the questions "How did you get here?" and "How will you move on?" She has awakened my spirit, restored my faith, and helped me understand the difference between the spiritual and physical realms. I feel empowered and more in control of my future. I feel better equipped to handle the life events that I'm sure I have yet to face. Terry reminded me that I've always had the power within me. Like Dorothy, I just never knew it, or knew how to apply it, or knew how easy it was to use.

I have always known the best teacher is one who has actually lived through the trials, has risen from the ashes, and shares his or her wisdom to help others. This is truly Terry fashion. Her concern for others' happiness has always been important to her. Terry definitely has her bona fide trials to share this incredibly insightful book with you.

Words cannot express how proud I am of her accomplishments and her approach to finding what is important inside each of us. She has not only learned from her difficult life experiences, but she wants to help you understand the power of happiness that rests within each of you.

It's no accident that you picked up *The Résumé of Life* by my friend— when the student is ready, the teacher appears. It doesn't matter why or how you found yourself in *your* situation; Terry will show you that you can profoundly move on! You will be inspired and motivated to change the outcome of your situation, whatever it may be. So, like Dorothy, realize that you have the power, and let Terry show you exactly how to tap into it.

I have been truly blessed to have Terry in my life for all these years. I am humbled to call her my friend. I cherish her friendship and love her more than she will ever know. I know that as you read this book, you too will get a sense of her wisdom, strength, and integrity and see that her brightness is brighter than ever!

Shelli Sherrill Lambert
Knoxville, Tennessee

INTRODUCTION

My name is Terry Walker. Although you may not know me in the physical sense, you do know me in the spiritual realm. We are all connected. We have all experienced life. The events we have experienced may differ, but the feelings are the same. Whether we experienced judgment, pain, shame, hurt, loss, anger, and rejection or experienced love, joy, peace, light, acceptance, and abundance, these experiences have all been a part of our journeys and the reason we are here. We have come to this physical realm to experience, to teach, to learn, to grow, to create, to share, to improve, and to help.

Ultimately, we are all here for a reason or a purpose. This is what I know and I believe. This book will help you to find your purpose and your truth. Once you recognize this, I promise your life will change for the better. Once you realize you can change your world and your way of being, the world around you will begin to change. This is an awakening, and I'm asking you not to push your snooze button on your alarm clock anymore.

This book was born by an awakening of understanding the difference between the physical world and the spiritual world. We all allow life (physical world) to get in the way. We all experience countless events throughout our lives. It's time to wake up and ask questions, allow for the answers, and open up to a knowing (spirit) to guide us to our purpose, or why we are here. *The Résumé of Life* will take you on a journey to open up and identify the differences between physical and spiritual. This book is entitled *The Résumé of Life* to help you better understand why you are here, what you have done in your life, and where you wish to go.

In the physical world, if you were to create your job résumé, it would need certain key elements:

- your contact information (who you are)
- your objective (what you want to do)

- your education (what you have learned)
- your work experience (what you have done)
- your skills and abilities (what you can do)
- your references (who knows you and what you are capable of doing)

The key elements all connect to show you are qualified for the job for which you are applying. You would build your job résumé to grow in your career, to seek a promotion, or to find a better job. Your résumé of life is much along the same level. You build your life résumé to grow, to learn, and to create a better life for yourself and others. As you create your job résumé, you may also review others' résumés as a sample to help remind you of things you might have missed or to establish a particular layout for your résumé. This should help you focus on your key points and attributes. When you have established your key points and your layout, your résumé should come into clearer focus and showcase your own experiences and talents. Much like a job résumé, *The Résumé of Life* was written to help you better understand who you are, what you have done, where you are now, and where you wish to go.

We all have alarm clocks in our lives that provide us with wake-up calls throughout our journeys, but do we continue to push the snooze button? *The Résumé of Life* will help you to identify experiences in your journey that may have changed the course of your direction. It will help you to wake up and become consciously aware of how your life experiences (your résumé) have led you to here and now.

Have you ever asked yourself these questions:

- How did I get to this place in my life?
- What events have led me to where I am now?
- Why am I here?
- What is my purpose?
- What have I gained or learned from my experiences?
- Do I continue to have experiences that lead to similar outcomes?
- How have I influenced others in my life?
- Have I ever been bullied, shamed, ridiculed, or judged?

- Have I ever been the one to bully, shame, ridicule, and judge others?
- How has this impacted my life or the lives of others?
- Do I live in fear and worry about not fitting in or other people's opinions of me?

As a sample résumé for you to review, I will offer you a glimpse into the résumé of my life. It is my hope that as you read my résumé, you will begin to relate portions, feelings, and experiences of my journey to those of your own. I hope it will inspire and motivate you to ask questions, just as I have done. I hope it will remind you of key events and experiences in your own life that will benefit you. Once you have reviewed my résumé, you and I will embark on a journey of faith, discovery, growth, and truth in an effort to bring your résumé into clearer focus. At the end of each chapter you will find blank pages titled Self-Reflection, for you to write your own notes and feelings that may have arisen as you read that chapter.

You have heard the phrase "mind, body, and spirit." We state it in that order: mind (ego, thoughts), body (our temple, our health, our appearance), and spirit (God, Spirit, universe, our soul, our energy, our space within where there is love, light, peace, balance, and truth.) You may have noticed on the cover of the book that I reorganized the statement to: "Spirit, Mind, and Body" (intentionally capitalized). I believe we need to understand that Spirit (God, universe, All That Is—however, you may refer to it) must come first. Once we put God first, then the mind (thoughts will change) and the body (temple, actions) will follow. That is the basis of this book. This is the awakening of life. This is *The Résumé of Life.*

We all have major events in our lives that change the course of our direction. We all have our crosses to bear. Our crosses are our burdens of pain, judgment, jealousy, fear, anxiety, worry, failure, anger, rejection, loss, abuse, and abandonment. On the other hand, we all have a soul, an inherent goodness of love, peace, freedom, joy, abundance, kindness, and truth. How many layers of burdens we pile upon our soul is how heavy our cross becomes before we awaken to the truth and let go or surrender these burdens.

I pray you will become more consciously aware of your spirit, your truth (purpose), your mind (thoughts), and your body (actions). I wish you love and light on your journey to the truth. I pray this book will inspire and motivate you to open up, to review, to create, and to enhance your résumé of life!

Namaste.

CHAPTER 1

Ground Zero

EVERYTHING HAS A STARTING POINT. Sometimes, to better understand the middle or the end of something, you need to know the starting point—ground zero.

This is my ground zero, and I am sharing it to offer you a glimpse into the résumé of my life. I do so in hopes that as you read these words you will be able to relate portions, feelings, and experiences of my journey to yours. As you read my résumé, I hope you begin to ask yourself questions, just as I have done, in an effort to bring your own résumé into clearer focus.

A Small-Town Girl

I grew up in a small town where everybody knew each other. If you also grew up in a small town, then you know that if you brought home someone new to meet the folks, you could rest assured that someone in your family either knew the other person's family or was a distant cousin to someone. Everyone always seemed to know somebody in the other person's family tree and was usually quick to enlighten the conversation with either positive or negative accolades. Again, we are all connected.

I grew up on a farm and had a good childhood. I enjoyed riding my horses and playing with my dogs and a variety of other pets. We lived next to my grandparents, and I spent a lot of time going back and forth between their house and ours. We shared the land and had a pond with a green bridge that connected the two properties. I kept that bridge hot, running back and forth between both homes. As a child, I remember knowing and thinking I was here for a reason. Although I never really understood what that thought meant, it remained throughout my childhood.

My grandfather reminded me of John Wayne, and we spent a great deal of time together, selling, trading, and showing horses. We would travel to stock sales and horse shows together. Some of my happiest childhood memories were when I was hanging with him and riding. He was a constant, strong figure in my life. He was a tall, strong man and the patriarch of our family. Even though he had a sixth-grade education, he was one of the smartest men I ever knew. When he was in his late seventies, he began searching for religion and God. We began to travel from church to church in search of whatever it was he had begun to look for. He began reading and studying the Bible and began questioning things about his life. He could barely read and write himself, but somehow he began to teach himself to read and comprehend. He did this through reading the Bible every day for hours, and in his own way, he would then meditate and think about what it meant. He began to write about what he was learning and make notes about the answers he felt he was coming to know. Over time, I began to see him changing and evolving. He began to read to my grandmother and me and ask us if we knew what the verses meant. As a child, I never really understood what he was trying to teach me, but it was here that I began to form a basis for spirituality. He began trying to teach us better ways of believing, knowing, and understanding.

At age thirteen, our house burned to the ground. It was an event that would change the course of my life. After the house burned, my parents decided we should move closer to town. This was a devastating time for me, as we would move away from the farm that I had grown up on and leave my grandparents and my animals behind.

Everything I was accustomed to in my life changed. My parents wanted me to be closer to school and friends and felt that I would be more involved with kids and activities for my age. It was a major change for me to leave the life I knew and loved. After the move, I adapted and enjoyed my friends and began to get involved in school activities and sports. However, I still missed the freedom of the country and being close to my grandparents and my animals.

What's the Point?

As I grew older, it was clear that I would go to college and be successful. The thought of knowing I was here for a reason somehow became buried with all the other things that began to transpire in my early adulthood. Life began to unfold. I went from being fairly popular in high school to going to college and not knowing anyone or really being anybody. I was just another person walking around on the college campus, wondering what in the world I was supposed to do with my life. I had no idea where I fit, what I wanted to do, or where I belonged. It was culture shock for me, and it was probably then that I began to lose myself. All I knew was to go to class and listen to specific subject matter, some of which I knew would never have a bearing on whatever I wanted to do as a career. I totally forgot that childhood belief of thinking I was here for a reason. I believe I began to lose my innate creativity and awareness of who I was. I had begun to listen to what others thought I should do and listen to the professors regarding what I was supposed to do to become successful.

The day finally came to graduate, and I began to have this crazy idea that since I had gone to college, I should be able to find a job immediately, start at least midlevel, and quickly rise to the top. After all, that's what the professors had stated, and that is why people spend years in college to obtain a degree, right? This was not the case, at least for me, and again, it was culture shock. I had graduated from college and had done what I had thought I was supposed to do to have a better job or career. Once I finished college, the world was supposed to open up for me. Again, that was not the case. Jobs were difficult to come by, and now that I had finished my degree, prospective employers would say that I didn't have any experience. How do you get experience if you can't find a job? Wasn't that why I spent those years in school for a degree, so I could have a better job?

I finally got a job that had nothing to do with my degree in mass communications and ended up working in the social arena with kids. I enjoyed the job and ended up furthering my education by going back to get my master's degree in educational psychology and counseling.

This became a turning point for me in my career and led me in a new direction that has helped me to understand more about the mind and human behavior. With this job, I felt that maybe I had found my niche. It was during the late 1980s that I moved back to my hometown, reestablished old friendships, and began to feel as though my life was finally coming together. I had also established a relationship that I was invested in. I cannot express how happy I had become. I had completed college, come back to my hometown, gone back to night school to work on my master's, reestablished friendships, finally found a job that I really enjoyed, and fallen in love. Things were falling into place for me. Ultimately, isn't that what we all seem to strive for: enjoying our lives; having someone to share our lives with; enjoying our jobs, our families, and our friends; and being able to make it on our own?

I felt as though I was finding my way in this world and my life was coming together. Along with my current job, I was also asked to sit on the board of directors for a new program being developed for children in the community. It was an exciting time for me; everything seemed to be falling into place. The person originally hired to run this new program ended up moving, and the board asked if I would consider taking the director position. I gladly accepted, left my current employment, and moved into the new position. I hit the ground running, and it was truly an exciting time. Even to this day, I can honestly say it was one of the most rewarding and favorite jobs I ever had.

Confrontation and Devastation

Suddenly, a day came when I was confronted about a rumor that I was gay. In that instant, everything changed. Isn't it ironic that everything you know or work to establish in your life can change or be taken away in an instant? This was a devastating confrontation. I was young, naïve, just beginning my career path, and didn't know what to do or how to respond.

I was put in a position to either lie about my personal life in an effort to keep my job or to be honest about my relationship and risk losing everything. I was told that if I denied the rumor, moved out of my current home, and lived by myself, then they would make the rumor go away and I could maintain my employment. In essence, they wanted me to lie about who I was, lie about whom I loved, remove myself from the home I was living in, and leave the relationship—all to keep my job. They gave me one no-win option: either leave my home and relationship or resign my position immediately.

I was scared and intimidated by the initial confrontation, but that was only the beginning. Since I did not resign on the spot or agree to move out of my home on the day of the confrontation, they gave me an option to go home to think about it for a couple of days and then return with my answer. A couple of days later, I met with them and refused to move out or end my relationship. I also refused to resign since they had no problems with my work ethic. At that point, they pulled me into a meeting behind closed doors and demanded my resignation or they would find a child to accuse me of abuse and take this to the media. What kind of person would threaten to coach a child to say that I had done something to try to harm that child? These types of threats were beyond comprehensible to me. In their opinion and fear-based thinking, because I was gay, I must also be a child abuser. What kind of person could do this to someone and even try to threaten to bring a child into the equation and coach that child to lie? There had been no performance issues with my job. In fact, I had helped to establish the program. But because of whom I loved and whom I was involved with on a personal level, they were threatening to go to such extremes to destroy my life and career.

I now know that people truly do judge and fear what they do not know or understand. During this process, they not only had their own fear, intimidation, and lack of awareness but did everything in their power to instill fear in me. I had gone to work every day, built a program for the children, and was appreciated for the work I had done. That is until they found out that I lived with another woman. Then I was nothing, and they were going to do whatever it took to destroy me.

I went from a wonderful job, furthering my education, and having a wonderful relationship to fear and hiding from people every time I went to the store. I was judged and treated as though I had the plague. I had no legal rights; I had nothing. I became afraid of seeing people in public and what they would think. People began to shun me. I would go to the store, and if I saw someone I knew going down an aisle, I would quickly bow my head and turn to go down an opposite aisle, hiding until I knew they were gone. I was afraid if they saw me that they would turn their back on me, ignore me, or worse, that they would begin threatening me. We had difficulty just going out to have dinner, for fear of running into someone and how they would treat us. The little things we take for granted—going out to dinner on a Friday night had now become a huge fear-based issue.

Soon, things began to spiral further out of control. They sent letters out to hold a public forum and threatened to write up an exposé in the local paper. These people belonged to a large local church and were very forthright in telling others about their affiliation. These same people attempted to destroy me over the fact that I lived with a person of the same sex. It absolutely had nothing to do with my work ethic but had everything to do with how I lived in my own home and with whom I chose to share my love and my life.

These people lived in judgment and fear. They took what they didn't know or understand and attempted to destroy a person's life because of it. I became angry and judgmental toward organized religion at that point in my life. My life had now become fear based, and I hid from everyone and everything I knew. They took me before the public forum, which was made up of people who knew my family and me. They had written letters and exposed my personal life to the community. I had to hire an out-of-town attorney to appear with me just to have some legal representation. I was taught to be kind and loving to everyone. My family instilled in me to have a good work ethic. I was taught to do the right thing. I was taught not to hurt or judge others, but the very people who claimed to be Christians were sure dropping their gavel of judgment down on me.

Once all of this began to surface throughout the town, my partner and I began to receive threatening phone calls. We were even physically attacked and beaten in a parking lot. They used a stun gun and tire jacks to beat us. My partner and I ended up in the back of an ambulance and taken to the emergency room to be treated. We were a bloody mess. The attackers ended up in the back of a police car, taken to jail and charged with attempted murder. If this wasn't enough, the local radio station announced it on air over the course of the next few days. Again, I was exposed. I had to appear in front of the grand jury that was also made up of people who knew my family and me. Eventually, I dropped the charges because I just could not take any more exposure, embarrassment, or pain than I had already endured. I could not bring any more attention, exposure, and shame to my family than they had already endured. This is what ignorance, hate, fear, and judgment can do. It spreads like a contagious disease and brings out the worst in people. Simply put, it destroys lives.

During all of this, I had now exposed my parents and my family to shame, embarrassment, and humiliation. How could this be? I felt I had done nothing wrong but felt that everyone had turned on me. I had nowhere to go and nowhere to hide. Everything was out in the open. My life was totally exposed. My parents tried to understand, and I knew they loved me, but they didn't deserve this. I didn't mean to embarrass or to hurt anyone, especially my family. I just wanted to live my life like everyone else—go to work, enjoy my new career, and be able to love the person that I wanted to share my journey with.

It was during one of the darkest times in my life that I looked out the window one day and saw my grandfather standing in the parking lot of my apartment building. I remember it just like it was yesterday. It was a clear day, sunny but cool, and there he was in his charcoal blazer over his western-cut shirt and suspenders, with his hat on and looking up at the apartment where I lived. I panicked! What was he about to say? What would he do? Was he coming to tell me that he no longer wanted me in his life? This was it; I could not have taken any more pain and rejection, and especially not from him. Within a couple of minutes, there was a knock on the door. I cannot begin to describe the anxiety and tension I felt as my heart fell into the pit of my stomach. I opened the door, and there he stood, this elderly, tall, strong man whom I loved and looked up to. Here was my John Wayne. He looked at me, smiled, and said, "I've come to talk to you." My partner was there, and he asked her to sit down with us. He wanted her to hear what he was about to say as well.

We sat down, and he began saying that he understood I had been through a lot and that he would never wish that on anyone and especially not his granddaughter. He had been very disappointed with how I had been treated, and he also said that he had built his own reputation, and for those who liked him, fine, and for those who didn't, that was fine too. He included both of us in the conversation as equals and spoke to us with kindness and thoughtfulness. He stated he loved me, and if this was what I wanted and it made me happy, then who was he or anyone else to try to tell someone whom they should love.

He didn't understand why this company was treating me this way since he had always told me, "It doesn't matter what you do in your job, but always do your best," and he was keenly aware of how hard I had worked in that position. He stated, "Even if you dig ditches, you be the best ditch digger there ever was, and no matter what position you hold, always treat others as equals."

Bless this eighty-four-year-old man, with minimal formal education, who tried his best to use appropriate terms in his conversation with us. He stated he did not know anything about homosexuality, but if that's how people loved one another, then who was he to judge it. He stated that he had come to realize over the years by living his life and by reading and studying the Bible that we are here to try to get along and to love one another. He said what he needed to say, got up, hugged my partner and me, and invited us over for dinner, and then he left. That was that! He came, he spoke of wisdom, love, and faith, and then he left. We were welcome in his house anytime, and he ended up spending many hours over the next few years with us discussing life and the Bible.

Somehow, over the next few months, I finished my master's program. However, looking back, I don't remember much about my graduation and my final exams because of the stress I was experiencing. I'm sure, though, it was God that carried me through it.

For all the anger, stress, and violence this brought into our lives, I began running and hiding from life. I ended up losing a five-year relationship and moved away from that town. I carried a great deal of anger, ran from myself, and distrusted everything and everyone for years after that event. I found no peace—no matter where I went. When I moved away, I ran to a place where no one knew me. I had no friends and found a temporary job that was just barely paying the bills. I gave up my life, my love, my home, and my new career. I was scared and felt alone. This was a major turning point in my life.

More Challenges, More Devastation

During the first year, I was able to find a job in the inpatient therapeutic field. The charge nurse hired me and took me under her wing. She was kind and supportive. We became friends, but still no one knew what I had been through and that I was running from pain, hurt, and judgment.

One day, a supervisor came to me and stated he would like to have a meeting with me that afternoon. He said he needed to work with me on some new restraint techniques. I went to his office at the scheduled time; he shut the door, flipped off the lights in his office, grabbed me from behind, and took me to the floor. He stated this was a "restraint technique" that I needed to learn. Here was my supervisor, a churchgoing, married man with a family, teaching me a "new technique," throwing me to the floor. At least, this is what he claimed. He refused to let me up and told me that he had been watching me on the unit and wanted more. Again, I was terrified. I had run from the one I loved, left my home, and lost my job and was now being told if I did not oblige, or if I ever told anyone what had happened, that he would ensure I would not work there much longer either. He stated that it would be his word against mine. He then let me up, and I left. A few days later, I opened up and told the charge nurse. I don't think she was surprised, as they had had suspicions but had not been able to prove anything. Within a few days, he quietly resigned his position, and I never saw him again. Isn't it ironic that people in power use intimidation and fear over others, all in the name of keeping your job?

Years later, I finally forgave them and attempted to let it go. Ultimately, you forgive. It doesn't matter about the person(s) you forgive; it matters about forgiving yourself. I had to forgive and let go of the anger, hurt, pain, fear, and distrust that I was carrying inside me. I carried it for years, and it only led me down paths of further chaos, negativity, and frustration. Until I finally let it go, it was difficult to move on in any direction. These were learning experiences that forever changed the course of my life and are ones that I will never forget.

I remained in the therapy field for another ten years. During that time, I was promoted on numerous occasions and recognized for my job performance. Due to health care and insurance changes, the last facility I worked for closed. Once again, I found myself moving in another career direction, but at least this time it had nothing to do with who I was, with whom I may have lived, or my job performance.

Around this time, my grandfather, who was now ninety-three years old, was still raising a garden and maintaining seven acres of farmland. One day he came in to cool off from working outside, slumped over in his chair, and passed away from a massive heart attack. This loss was devastating for my entire family and me. He had always been there for all of us. I guess I never, ever thought of my life without him. It was unimaginable to me that he was gone. After all the painful events I had endured, this was by far the most painful. I remember as we drove through town with the funeral procession that people stepped outside their businesses to watch it pass by and to pay their respects. It was a beautiful sight and one I am grateful for; it was fitting for such a wonderful, well-respected man. However, I also remember thinking in my mind, *How can anybody go on with their lives if Pappaw isn't here?* I know now that he is here with my family and me always. After many years of running, I have come back full circle to what he tried to teach me and the things he tried to help me understand. He tried to instill an awareness of spirituality, truth, and conscious understanding. Although I did not begin to use it or understand it until the past few years, this was where it started, and I carried it with me until I was ready to awaken to it.

A few years after my grandfather passed, I sustained a closed-head injury. I sustained a skull fracture and bruising of my brain in a significant event. I had both long-term and short-term memory loss. I also severed my olfactory nerve and lost my sense of smell. My speech was very slow, and I cried a lot. I knew what was going on around me, but I could not effectively carry on a conversation. I saw my family and friends look at me with fear in their eyes, wondering if this was how I was going to remain. Would I be able to function and communicate effectively or even hold down a job? I had to begin the road of recovery, rebuilding, and rediscovering who I was. Here again was another turning point in my life, as I had to relearn basic things and regain a sense of self.

A New Journey

After the hospital I had worked for closed and my head injury started to heal, a very good friend helped me to secure a job in the medical field. The job helped me to be able to maintain paying my bills until I found something else. Almost fourteen years later, I'm still with that company and in sales. I enjoy the opportunity to get out, meet new people, present and discuss new information, and help others. However, over the past few years, the long-lost childhood belief of being here for a reason has begun to resurface. I've begun to wonder and ask the question, "How did I get here?" The belief of being here for a reason has grown more prevalent over the past couple of years, along with life getting in the way and all the difficulties that have taken place. I know there is something more. I've started to ask soul-searching questions:

- What is happiness?
- What is the American dream, and is there really such a thing?
- Why do some people seem to be fulfilled, happy, and able to follow their dreams and I am not?
- What are my dreams?

I felt as though I had no creativity, no focus, and no true happiness. Somewhere I had lost this creativity and joy over the years. I'd lost the childhood wonder, the truth of being; I had lost my purpose. I felt alone, and I felt as though I had lost myself. I had friends, and I had people who cared, but deep down, I felt struggle. Something was not right, and I didn't know what it was. Financially, I was doing fairly well. I had a nice house and a good job but still felt as though something was missing. I was still concerned about what others thought of me and who I was. What was all of this for if deep down there was still that feeling of being alone and unfulfilled? My concerns were based on things and events outside of myself that only seemed to perpetuate the emptiness I felt on the inside.

I was overweight, and my health was declining because I was not taking care of myself. Whenever I was asked to go out and do things, it was a struggle. No matter where I went, there I was. I couldn't find me, and if I glimpsed at myself, I sure didn't like what I saw. Many years ago, I used to be very outgoing and the life of the party, but that seemed like a lifetime ago. I used to enjoy my life and activities, but now I couldn't seem to find any joy. All I knew was if I agreed to go and do anything, it was a struggle. If I did go somewhere, I could only *try* to enjoy myself but mostly couldn't wait to go back home. I felt alone at home, and I felt alone when I was out with friends. It was during this time my mother was diagnosed with stage 3 ovarian cancer. My parents and I are very close, so this was a very difficult blow to my family. However, she remained strong and positive, and I am proud to say she is a survivor!

A Bump in the Road

I am happy to tell you that my life hasn't been all bad. After the death of my grandfather, my mother's diagnosis, and getting a job that I enjoy, I met a wonderful woman and fell in love again! We were together for twelve years, and being with her provided me the opportunity to have my own family. I had a partner, and she gifted me with sharing and raising her son. This relationship and our son provided me with so much joy during those years. I had the opportunity to watch him grow up and mature into a spectacular young man. We may not have been your typical family (whatever that is these days), but we were a family. This was my family, the one with whom I shared my daily life and love. Her family also accepted me as a member of the fold without hate and judgment. It gave me a sense of stability and stopped me from running. I began to trust and feel accepted by someone, and it gave me a positive focus.

We were like any other family. We would go to work, spend time as a family, pay bills, go on vacation, and share our lives. We built a new house, and it was a weekend tradition that our son would have his friends over to hang out and play. We would grill out or order pizza, and they would stay up all night playing games, laughing, and watching movies.

After twelve years, the day came when she met someone else. In an instant, it was over. The loss was devastating. I felt as though I did not matter and had easily been replaced. I was alone, devastated, and empty. I'd lost my partner and my son and was no longer a member of her family. Everything I had worked for and believed in was gone in an instant. My family was gone. After all of the other events and losses I had endured, this one was the final straw. I just wasn't sure if I could or would be able to bounce back. I felt as though everything I had built, worked for, and believed in was gone. I felt as though a tornado had come through my life, and everything was demolished. There was nothing left standing.

As an adult, I've experienced struggle, pain, loss, and judgment. I guess all of this was truly taking a toll on my spirit, mind, and body. I wondered why I was here and if I even mattered. Why should I care or even try anymore? I had lost faith in everything, in everyone, and certainly in myself. My weight was continuing to spiral out of control, and that didn't help to influence me to be in the public either. I just didn't know where I fit. I always worried what others thought of me. I worried about their opinions on what I should be doing. I just wanted to be loved and accepted. Everything had become a struggle. It was difficult to function, to work, and to take care of myself and my home.

After losing my relationship, the losses somehow kept coming. I worried about how I maybe didn't measure up and again worried about others' opinions. At the time, it was a devastating blow, but now I realize it was for the best. The relationship had become stagnant, and neither of us was moving; neither of us was growing or flowing. This feeling of struggle within me was also continuing to grow stronger. Today, I recognize the relationship needed to end to allow for both of us to continue on our journeys and to move forward with our lives. It had fulfilled its purpose, and now it was time for more. When I was immersed in the pain of it all, I certainly could not see any of this at the time, but I do know it now.

Time heals, but that's exactly what it takes—time. I now recognize that we have to continue to grow on our journeys, and when it is time for more, we will receive it whether we want it or not. That didn't take away all the pain that was associated with the loss, but it did provide me with the opportunity to begin a new path and to begin to grow again.

Wake-Up Calls

As I mentioned earlier, there is a purpose, a knowing, a truth as to why we are here on this physical plane. I had the joy of a family and a son. In essence, I now know it was never lost. It just had to take on a new form. However, there is more to do, more to learn, and more to become. During that devastating period, something kept me going every day. My energy was depleted, but somehow I kept going. I turned to faith, as that's all I knew I could do. There was no energy left for me to run and hide anymore. God sat me down so that I could finally begin a new journey of awareness and growth. My choices were to continue to wallow in the pain and destruction, to run and search for someone or something else to fill the void, or begin to find me and begin healing and growing. We cannot see this when we are wrapped up in the fear, the pain, the loss, or the rejection of it all. However, if we take time to realize and believe that everything happens for a reason and find our faith within, we can and will get through it. We must learn, grow, and carry on. I had been humbled. When one door closes, another door must open. I had been given another wake-up call, and this time I didn't have the energy to run away or even try to push my snooze button.

One day, I was lying in bed with the worst flu that I ever remember having in my life. I had been so sick and weak that I had difficulty gaining enough energy to walk across the room. I remember lying in bed watching TV. I flipped to the PBS Channel where Dr. Wayne Dyer was discussing his book *Change Your Thoughts, Change Your Life*. I watched the show, made myself get out of the bed, went to the local bookstore, and bought the book. I'd like to think of this as another one of my wake-up calls. I began reading, studying, and trying to find some meaning in my life.

I soon began to exercise by walking. Within nine months, I lost forty pounds and entered a half marathon. During this time, I began to learn more about the importance of self-affirmations. As I began to walk, I would state affirmations to myself, such as "I am healthy," "I am abundant," "I am love," "I am light," and so on. During the walks, I would replay these affirmations in my mind until I started to feel and believe them. I was becoming stronger, and my energy was improving.

A year later, I got sick again with a severe infection and became extremely ill. The doctors were concerned enough about the fevers I was experiencing that they decided to run tests for cancer. This was another health blow, and it was scary for me since I was alone at the time. It was then I feel I had another wake-up call. A few months later, my father became extremely ill, and that was another wake-up call. I was trying to remain strong for him and my mother, and I thank God I had rebuilt enough energy to do that.

At this point, with life continuing to happen, I wasn't walking as much and felt my weight begin to creep back up. A good friend of mine had been discussing a personal trainer with me over the past year, but I had so much going on I just wasn't willing to allow for anything or anyone new. I didn't need help. I thought I knew what I was doing. I didn't need someone to tell me how to exercise or to lose weight. After all, I'd completed a half marathon. In my younger years, I had worked out and played sports. How dare anybody try to offer advice or help! Looking back on that now, I wasn't ready. I was still struggling with trying to fix things myself. After all, look at all I had done. I had lost weight with my walking and completed a half marathon, and I did it all on my own, or so I thought. One day, my friend brought the trainer conversation back up again, and for whatever reason, I decided immediately I would give it a try. However, we needed to do it now or never. Patience has never been my strong suit, and I've always been the kind of person that once I decide on something, I want it now. No waiting, just do it. And so it happened. I was finally ready.

Finally Ready for Change

I received a call from the trainer and interviewed her over the phone. Whatever I threw at her in the conversation, she remained supportive and kind. Thinking about it now, I was still carrying anger and distrust within because I was still trying to control and fix it myself. I probably wasn't the easiest call she'd ever made. She seemed to say the right things and had the answers to what I guess I needed to hear. She seemed to understand and relate to what I wanted to do. I decided to give her a chance. She came to my house and answered questions, discussed nutrition, and told me what she could do to help me. We set goals, and I went with it. Shortly after that meeting, I was talking to a friend on the phone and vividly remember saying, "I don't know where this is going, but I know it's going somewhere. I'm surrendering this to God, and I'm just going to go with it." Another wake-up call, and this time I was surrendering and allowing for help.

A few months later, I found myself working more closely with my trainer and beginning to establish trust in someone again. Trust was something I had lost a long time ago. Always supportive, she would answer my questions or concerns, and I began to trust in what she said. After all, the results were beginning to speak for themselves. She was teaching me the importance of nutrition and exercise. She was helping me to become stronger and to accomplish things I never dreamed possible. I was amazed at what was happening to my body and my self-confidence. We would have in-depth discussions during our workouts, and she became a godsend in my life. I have now realized that when I was ready and surrendered to allow myself to be open to new possibilities, God provided the right person at the right time. I was learning to focus and to trust in the process. I dropped four sizes in my clothes. All this was a great accomplishment as my mind and body were transforming. However, what I didn't realize was that the spiritual side of me still needed to transform as well.

Faith, Surrender, Allow

At this point, I began to wonder what was taking place in my life. All I knew was to keep my focus and believe there was a reason behind all of it. Three words began to sustain me: faith, surrender, and allow. One phrase began to resonate as well: "Trust in the process." Those were the words I felt I was hearing from within, and so that's what I did. I somehow knew it was all a part of the process and would lead me to more.

After months of training, physical transformation, and growth, I began to feel as though there was still something nagging at me. What could it be? I had begun to let go of my lost relationship, the pain, the anger, the rejection, and the hurt. I thought that I had forgiven the ones I felt hurt me throughout my past. I was grateful for my accomplishments, and my health and physique were much improved.

However, there was still something within me that still was not quite right. I still didn't know where I fit. I still wasn't big on the idea of going out with others, and it still felt like a struggle. I refer to this as a process of trying to clean out my basement. I had come a long way, but there was still something over in a dark corner in the basement that I just couldn't quite understand. I just couldn't shine a light on it. I still had some struggle or pain, something hidden over in the corner that I just couldn't reach.

When the Student Is Ready …

I had begun the process of learning and feeling gratitude, and I was grateful for the gifts I had begun to recognize in my life. I was grateful for my health, my job, my home, my family, and my friends, and I had read that gratitude was extremely important to verbalize and feel. Still, there was something wrong. What could it be that was still holding me? I knew I wasn't depressed. I'd come so far and was so very grateful. I had begun to find me, the happiness within me, and yet there was still something holding me. Still some type of struggle and pain. I was still holding on to something but could not quite reach it. Again, could this be another wake-up call? What was I missing? I was still reading my spiritual books, but I was feeling stuck.

One day I'd had a tough week at work and was feeling tired and drained. I could feel my energy was low, and for some reason I had an intense sadness that day. I went for a drive and saw a church on the corner with a sign that read: "If God says it, it must be so." I turned down the road just past that sign and thought about that statement for a moment, even said it aloud, and then let it go. I drove further and saw another sign on the road that caught my attention. At that point, something kept telling me to turn around and go back. I drove a little further, thinking, *This is crazy*, but there was that struggle again, and it seemed more intense than ever. I drove a few more miles, but there was a voice inside me saying, "Terry, turn around and go back." At that point, the voice kept getting louder and more prevalent, and I guess the pain and frustration finally got the best of me, so I turned the car around and went back. Over the years, I had read about paying attention to the signs that show up on your path—so this time, I decided to pay attention.

I pulled in the parking lot and sat there still struggling with whether or not to get out of the car. There was a phone number on the sign, so I called it and got a voicemail. I quickly hung up and put the car in reverse to pull out of the parking lot. As I was getting ready to pull out of the lot, the voice got stronger, and the struggle I was feeling got more intense. Something kept saying to call the number back and at least leave a message. I bargained with that voice and decided that if I left a message and if someone called back later, and I didn't want to talk, then I could just say I had changed my mind. At least I would make an effort to call back if it would somehow stop this voice from hounding me about it.

I parked the car and made a second call and was all prepared to leave my number when this time a woman answered the phone … now what? I had to say something or just hang up. This was not the recorded message that I had bargained for hearing. There was a person on the other end of the line waiting for me to say something. I spoke with her and asked some questions about her practice. She stated she was on her way to the office and would be there within thirty minutes. I agreed to come back and meet with her, and now I am so grateful I did. This was the day I met a woman whom I affectionately refer to as my spiritual adviser. Again, I had surrendered to an inner voice, and I believe this was God bringing another person in my life at the right time for the right reason.

I was feeling an intense pain and sadness that day and could not understand why. It was at that moment I let go of any preconceived notions, judgment, or opinions and allowed myself to open up and listen. I'm sure you've heard the statement "Don't ask the question if you are not prepared for the answer." My question, along with my reason for asking, was "Why am I still feeling this pain and struggle within?" I had been reading my spiritual books, and I had continued to work out, but it still wasn't enough. I needed to know! I couldn't understand what was going on within me.

She introduced herself, and I saw and felt a gentleness and kindness in her eyes that seemed to say I was right where I needed to be, and everything was going to be okay. After we began to talk, one of the first statements she made was, "I can tell you are a spiritual person, but why are you questioning it?" There it was. It was all out in the open, and her statement hit me like a ton of bricks. Something I just couldn't reach in my basement and the one thing I had done all my life was worry about others' opinions and allow those opinions to define me.

I did believe in God, the universe, whatever word you use to refer to a higher being, but I still questioned everything. Also, I had never believed in myself. If I did not believe in myself and worried about everyone else's opinions, then how could I truly believe in God? If I listened to everyone else, how could I listen to God—the voice within? I had forgotten why I was here. I had lost me; I had lost my purpose. I had turned everything over to physical, outside entities. I mentioned issues earlier with trust, but my greatest downfall was not trusting in me, and worst of all, that meant I was not trusting in God, in Spirit.

She stated I was like someone in a movie with an angel on one shoulder and a devil on the other, and it was as though I didn't know which way to turn. I was still questioning my faith. It was at that moment the doors flew open for me, and someone finally seemed to pinpoint exactly what I was feeling. And for the first time I felt the light come on and flicker in that dark corner of my basement! I truly believe that this was my next wake-up call in the process of the journey I had embarked on almost two years earlier.

I had gone through the physical transformation; now it was time to work on the spiritual transformation. I worked out my physical muscles; now it was time to work out and build my spiritual muscles. It all made sense. I surrendered again to allow God to bring the right person in my life at the right time. I let go of hurt, anger, deceit, and struggle and began to open up and allow for help. I had reached a point that I knew there had to be more, and there was still something that needed work inside of me. I realized that it was something that I alone could not fix. I had known I was here for a purpose and was finally remembering that belief from my childhood.

I have known for years that I was to write a book and wanted to be a motivational speaker. However, it was a dream of mine, and I figured it was just something I may or may not achieve. I've done some speaking on a small scale, and I recognize that when I speak, I feel a love and transformation that is a high I've never been able to obtain in any other way. If you have ever done anything you were extremely passionate about, you know that feeling.

I wanted to write a book but never knew exactly what I wanted to say. Once I explained this to my new acquaintance, her question was, "If you don't know, then how can you write or speak about it?" No one had ever stated such a thing to me, but it was true, and I knew it. This was the moment of surrender. I had to allow for help once again. This was the beginning of another new connection with someone whom I needed to trust and to allow to work with me. I needed to stop questioning my faith! I needed to ask God and then surrender to God—to Spirit—to help me continue on my journey and find my purpose.

She talked to me about the Bible, faith, and acceptance. She talked to me about how to pray and how to meditate. She taught me how to go within, to listen and to believe. She helped me to understand that not all organized religions are judgmental and bad. She helped me to remember what my grandfather had tried to teach and instill in me so many years ago. She told me that my grandfather is here with me and that he had left me something. What he left me wasn't of material value, but she felt he wanted to know if I had received it. I couldn't imagine what it was, but I have often wondered what it could be.

Throughout this process, I have now come to believe that there truly is a power that is greater than we are, and all we have to do is surrender and allow it to heal us. We all have it. We are all connected, and if we open ourselves up to this awareness, our lives will change.

I'm Just Like You ... You're Just Like Me

I have given you a glimpse of my life and hope you will understand that I am just like you. I have carried these burdens for many years, and now I am surrendering to the truth. No matter what I went through, no matter how alone or fearful I felt, no matter how far I seemed to run from one thing to another, trying to find acceptance, love, peace, and happiness, the truth is that I was never alone. God never left; it was me who continued to run and hide or to fix or handle everything myself. I often use the phrase, "No matter where you go, there you are." I wouldn't surrender. I just kept moving and going from one thing to another.

We all have our lives to live, paths to walk, and experiences to live, but the one constant is we have a soul: an inherent goodness that we can surrender our burdens to at any given moment. My grandfather always used to say that God is patiently waiting, and all we have to do is allow him to come into our lives. He also had a phrase: *faith believin'*. He would use those phrases to help sustain how he was feeling and to provide some sense of strength in a particularly challenging moment. As I began to remember and recognize his teachings and phrases, I began to grow. I began using his statements and established my own phrases as well.

Throughout this glimpse of my ground zero—the résumé of my life that I've chosen to share with you—I hope you see that I am just like you. I have experienced loss, struggle, rejection, abandonment, unemployment, and weight and health issues, and I have been judged on my lifestyle. I have also experienced love, joy, peace, truth, abundance, and happiness. I have felt the struggle within and have felt a pull that there must be more. Maybe the actual events I've shared with you are not the same as yours, but the outcomes and feelings are likely similar.

I truly believe that everything happens at the right time for the right reason. I have lived it, and now I am sharing it with you. We are given road signs along the way in our lives; some call it a gut feeling, some call it intuition, some call it an inner voice, and some call it a knowing or a feeling. Whether we listen to that inner voice or not is up to the free will that God gave us, but rest assured the reward or consequence of that choice will soon make itself known. Just remember the saying, "The truth shall prevail."

CHAPTER 2

The Baby Effect

AFTER REVIEWING MY RÉSUMÉ, I hope it has inspired you to ask questions and begin to review, focus, and enhance your résumé. As with your employment résumé, what is the first thing you would put on your résumé? Contact information! We all arrive here with our own contact information, which goes something like this: we arrive on this earthly plane in the physical form of an infant. On the outside, it may seem like we arrive with nothing more than the DNA of our parents and the name they gave to us. I believe we come here with so much more.

We are all born with an inner knowing. This knowing is something that guides us through our infancy and is part of our entire life. We may not remember our infancy and growth process until, as adults, we observe babies as they grow.

It does not matter what language you speak, because babies do not understand words or the meaning of words. However, babies do understand and let us know in their own way when they are hungry, wet, sick, or happy. They let us know when they need attention, help, and comfort. As a baby grows and becomes stronger, you may walk into her room one morning and find she has pulled herself up and is standing and holding on to the side of the crib. You didn't teach the baby to stand, nor did you tell the baby to stand. Sheer instinct let the baby know when she was strong enough and when it was time to pull herself up and stand in the crib. This is an internal clock, a knowing inside that baby that told her when it was time to pull herself up at that particular moment and on that particular day. It is that same internal clock and knowing that is in each of us.

After the baby learns to stand, it is only a matter of time before she takes her first steps. With the first steps, the baby will fall, and it may scare her and cause some tears. However, she doesn't stop trying or quit for fear of falling. She will get up again, take a step or two, and fall again.

Before you know it, the steps turn into a quick trot to include more falls and maybe a few more fearful tears. However, the baby does not allow fear to overpower her. Nor does fear stop the baby from getting back up, trying again, learning to walk, and eventually running.

As you see, even in infancy, we took some falls, but something inside us kept us moving and continuing to gain strength to get back up and try again. As we observe the baby gaining confidence and strength, we remain supportive and loving. We motivate the baby to become stronger, more confident and self-assured than she was initially. I've never heard an adult trying to motivate a baby to walk by saying, "You can't walk. You're not strong enough. Don't do that, or you'll get hurt!" We don't instill fear and try to discourage the child. On the contrary, we continue to encourage and help the baby to walk. We support, motivate, and comfort the baby to get back up and try again even when she falls and sheds fear-based tears.

What happens next? When did we stop encouraging the child during his or her growth process? When did we instill fear and lack of trust? When did we, as adults, learn to stop trusting ourselves and to stop following our dreams, our knowing, and our purpose?

The baby has an internal clock and knowing that lets him know when it's time to pull himself up and begin to walk. I've never heard a baby say, "I fell; it scared me, and I give up." Or, "I'm afraid, and I'm never going to attempt to walk again!" This internal clock, this strength, this knowing is in all of us. No one can predict that on a certain day at a certain time, a baby will take his first steps. However, we do know there are points and milestones that come at particular times in the baby's life. This is true throughout our entire life. We go through milestones in our life: infancy, childhood, puberty, early adulthood, adulthood, and the aging process. We are physically aware of these milestones in another person's life. However, when do we begin to awaken to our own spiritual internal knowing? What happened to that same spiritual internal knowing we had as infants? How many times have we pushed our snooze button on our alarm clock? When did we begin to allow external influences to override our knowing?

When we arrive here as babies, we have no concept of the physical world, such as money, cars, electronics, brand names, and so on. We also have no concept of hate, judgment, finances, greed, power and control, race, religion, or sex. We only know that we need love, nurturing, acceptance, and caring.

As the baby gets older, we go to the store and cannot go down an aisle without him pointing to and wanting everything in the store. He still has no concept of money, brand names, or material things. He is simply observant and aware of colors, shapes, sounds, and so on. This is the beginning of physical wants and the thinking that if he can have this one toy, it will make him happy. As adults, we may tell the baby he doesn't need it. If we choose to purchase that toy to make him happy, we know the child might be happy with the toy at that moment, but in reality, the happiness for that one toy will not last. Soon, there will be something else the child wants that will be *the one thing* that will make him happy. We know this to be true about that toy for the child. However, as adults, do we do the same thing in search of happiness? Do we search outside ourselves for happiness on a much larger scale, be it cars, material possessions, and even relationships? We think these physical, exciting new toys or new people will complete us, make us happy and get us noticed. Could we be confusing these physical wants as an external quest to find love, happiness, and acceptance? In reality, the new toys may provide some sense of happiness, but will that happiness last?

As our lives progress, we experience the physical world and the effects of the world. This is when we may begin to push our snooze button on our alarm clock and stop listening to our inner knowing, our spirit. We get caught up seeking outside worldly possessions to help us feel complete. We seem to stop listening to our spirit, our guide, and we lose focus on our purpose. Hence, many of us begin to focus on things outside ourselves and lose focus on what is inherent.

We stand in our own way and sabotage our lives. We allow others to impose their opinions of us. We believe we cannot do something because of what someone else thinks or tells us. We even tell ourselves that "I can't" or "I'm afraid" or "I'm not capable or good enough." This type of thinking will continue to manifest into failure. When did we stop trusting and listening to our inner knowing, our truth, and begin to allow for self-sabotage, fear, and doubt? With self-doubt, nothing gets accomplished, and our lives remain in fear, struggle, and stagnation. It is difficult to grow or find true happiness if this is how you have come to believe. These are all things taught to us by the outside physical world.

The baby does not know he cannot walk when the time comes to walk. He just pulls himself up and begins to take the first steps. As adults and parents, we don't try to discourage the baby from walking. Nor do we interject fear or hate into the baby and try to discourage him from walking. We provide love and support to encourage the baby to continue to try to walk. Again, where did this love and encouragement go for us? When did we begin to allow others to change our contact information? Do we try to stand in the way of others' dreams? Do we sabotage our own dreams? When did we stop listening to our internal knowing, our self-love, and begin listening to others outside of us? When did we push aside our sense of knowing? When did we begin to believe that the things outside of us are what make us who we are and get us noticed? When did we begin to live in fear of our life, our purpose, and ourselves? When did we stop believing in why we are here and who we truly are?

SELF-REFLECTION

(This space is provided for you to reflect on how you can apply what you've read.)

CHAPTER 3

Wants versus Needs

AS WE CONTINUE TO REVIEW your contact information on your résumé, it is time to consider wants versus needs in your life. We need to understand if our wants are provoking a sense of entitlement. As we grow in this physical school called life, we begin to leave our true selves behind and look for things that we believe will get us attention and acceptance. We want the latest video games, newest phone, fancy car, big home, brand-name clothing, and so on. We feel that these expensive, new, shiny things make us who we are or who we are trying to become. Oftentimes, we use these external wants of the physical world to seek attention, happiness, and acceptance.

However, if we take an honest look at our wants versus our needs, our wants may begin to take on a different meaning. Our needs are as follows: food, shelter, clothing, and a sense of love, acceptance, and belonging. We need food to survive. We need shelter. We need clothes. However, our greatest longing is for love, acceptance, and belonging. We need love and acceptance to feel complete. No amount of material wealth or possessions can fill our deep-seated need for love and acceptance. Our spirit, our true self, is where and how we are all connected. We need to provide love and to accept love in an effort to feel that we truly matter. We are here to experience love, to give and to receive love, to have a sense of connection, acceptance, and belonging. We are here to grow, experience, and improve upon things while in this physical form. If we fail to establish and awaken to the love, acceptance, peace, and truth within ourselves, how can we give it or even feel worthy of receiving it? We must begin with our spirit (our own love and acceptance), and then we will become what we wish to be and obtain what we wish to have in this life.

If we continue to search outside of ourselves and purchase things that we feel will make us happy, that feeling of happiness will never last. If we choose to continue to believe the lie that it will, our lives will continue to cycle out of control, and likely so will our finances. Why? Because there will always be newer electronics, newer cars, more name-brand clothing—all of which push us further into debt and keep us from obtaining a true sense of love and belonging. We also may find ourselves running from one person to another in an effort to find that special person who will complete us or make us whole. All of this is still searching on the outside looking for something that we already have on the inside. This vicious cycle keeps us seeking outside ourselves for more and more in an effort to find love, belonging, acceptance, peace, and joy. However, by doing this, we move further away from our true selves—our inner knowing—and lose the truth of who we really are. We begin to find ourselves in more struggles, more pain, and more anxiety. The struggles and the pain can cause us to create bigger debt or bigger promises. Then we discover our limited abilities—whether to pay the debt or keep the one person who we thought would complete us. We realize—sometimes when it is too late—that we cannot make good on the debt or the person.

No amount of money, sex, partners, alcohol, drugs, or material things will complete us and give us a true, lasting sense of happiness. If you do not find love, peace, and joy from within, you cannot give it, and you cannot truly receive it. You must stop running and searching for everything outside of yourself, looking for what you already possess internally. As I stated in "The Baby Effect," you had it when you arrived on this earthly journey, and it has never left or forsaken you.

Sometimes we forget and get caught up in the trappings of the physical world. We have also defined ourselves and who we are by others' opinions of us. It's based on our job title, our wealth, our home, our physical appearance, our family, our car, or the latest gadget we have. As I mentioned earlier, these are on the physical realm and can never bring us true, lasting happiness, love, acceptance, and peace of mind. Instead, they keep us in a constant state of worry, debt, and struggle, searching for a way to hold on to them, only to replace them when the newness wears off. Sadly, we are the hamster running on the hamster wheel!

What if you had acquired all of these things and they suddenly were removed from you? How would you feel if you were stripped bare of people, places, and things? How would you identify yourself then? What would you have? Who would you be? Were you truly grateful for those people, places, and things when they were with you? We use material possessions to identify and define ourselves on the physical realm. These material things can't love us; nor can they provide us with a feeling of acceptance. The physical is not who we truly are! An item or a person cannot make us whole or complete. It is our purpose to become whole and complete within our own selves. We need to believe in, to expand upon, to share ourselves, and to be grateful for who we truly are. Once we recognize this and build our spiritual muscle, the world around us will begin to improve and change.

We have gotten ourselves into a tremendous amount of debt in our own households by seeking, buying, and living beyond our means. Why? We're simply trying to fit in or to find happiness. However, when the bills come in, we find ourselves struggling and full of anxiety trying to pay them. Think about this: When the bills come due, and we have to pay, where is the happiness and joy from the purchase we made? Did this purchase bring us love and acceptance? I know a few people who have taken on a second job because they were living in fear of how they could pay these bills. This anxiety and struggle takes away from our sense of well-being, our truth, and even our families! If we get back to the basics of fulfilling our needs, building our strength, our love, and our peace within, we will change the way we see things, and everything around us will change, as well. It's time to get back to and listen to our internal knowing that we arrived here with—that knowing that has been with us all along.

We must let go of this sense of entitlement and take responsibility for who we are and where we are right here and now. We need to get out of our own way and establish our own truth, acceptance, and love. We are angry with the government for the debt that has accrued in this country. They too have taken us down a road filled with a sense of entitlement and living beyond their means. We say we don't want to pass this government debt down to our children. But in essence, what are we doing in our own homes and our own lives to take care of our own selves, our own families, and our own bills? If we can't take care of our own finances and our own truth, how can we expect others to do it for us? We must begin to change our own world individually and recognize the difference in our own lives.

If we get back to needs and basics, we may begin to see we have more money to do things we enjoy that do not require living beyond our means. We will be kinder, loving, accepting, and grateful of others and ourselves. We will have more peace, balance, and joy with less worry or struggle. We will have more qualitative and quantitative time to spend with our family. We will have more gratitude for what we currently have rather than always seeking and searching for more. We may find our finances, our peace, and our love will improve. The struggles and anxiety will begin to dissolve. We will begin to love and accept ourselves, to have love and acceptance for others, and in turn, it shall return to us multiplied. What would this world be like if we as individuals recognized these things, began to take responsibility for our own lives, and got our own selves in a better place? Truly, it takes a village, and it begins with you.

I invite you to get a pen and paper and begin your notes for your résumé. What aspects of this book, thus far, have begun to resonate with you? What awareness has opened up for you? These are your notes, your truth, and your awakening that you are experiencing while relating to these chapters. We've touched on growth and awareness, wants and needs, finances, and anything else you may have awakened to in your life. This is your contact information. Honesty, truth, and responsibility are now in your hands as you make notes on your résumé of where you have been, where you are now, and where you wish to go.

SELF-REFLECTION

(This space is provided for you to reflect on
how you can apply what you've read.)

CHAPTER 4

Free Will

WHILE WE ARE ON THIS earthly journey, we have been given free will. For your résumé, this corresponds to your objective of what you want to do. We've been given free will (choices) to do with our lives and to live our lives however we choose. We make numerous choices every single day. Some of our choices may be simple, and some may be complex. Many of the choices we make each day are so simple and routine that we don't even realize we make them. For example, we have the choice to get up each morning, brush our teeth, shower, and go to work. Most of us do this as part of our daily routine and don't think twice about it. However, even the simplest choice of brushing our teeth can lead to either rewards or consequences. For every action, reaction, and choice, there is a consequence or reward. If our objective is to have good oral hygiene, the reward will be better health, better dental checkups, and positive feelings of self. If we choose not to care for our teeth, the consequence will result in poor health and tooth decay and may even affect our feelings of self-worth.

This analogy may sound simplistic, but if you are unaware of even the simplest choices you make on any given day, how can you understand and identify the more complex choices? To identify and look at your résumé, you have to understand your objective and become more consciously aware of your choices in your daily life.

It's time to look at you and stop pointing the finger or blame at someone else. It's time to look at you and your objective and stop worrying about others' opinions. Anything from here on is for you. You have to learn that everything comes from within, and you must become clear on your objective and begin to make conscious choices about who you are, where you are, and where you want to go. This is the free will God has given to us.

We have our soul, our instinct, our knowing, and we also have our mind, our ego, and our thought process. As I described in "The Baby Effect," we come here with our soul, our knowing, and our purpose. As we grow and go through life in the physical realm, we begin to communicate more readily from our mind, our ego, and our thought processes rather than our soul (our instinct or our knowing). We tend to forget that our soul knows why we are here. Our soul knows our purpose and our needs. However, as we grow, we begin to make decisions more readily with our mind (ego) and our wants.

We have come into the age of computers and social media. This has been a good thing, as we have begun to evolve as a society, but it can also be detrimental to our being. Maybe you've heard the statement: garbage in, garbage out. Simply put, computers only know the information we program into them. The information that's been programmed into computers is information we can easily look up and quickly access. Some of the information may be correct, educational, and even worthwhile, while some information may be incomplete, negative, or worthless. Computers are not human; they do not have feelings, and they don't have a sense of knowing.

I believe that our minds are similar to computers. If we program our minds and our thoughts with fearful, negative, angry, judgmental information, then that is what we will put into the world. If we choose to live in fear, anger, judgment, struggle, and hatred, then we will live a life filled with fear, anger, judgment, struggle, and hatred. On the other hand, if we choose to live a life of love, peace, balance, abundance, and harmony, which comes from our soul and not our mind, then we will surround ourselves with this way of being. It's your choice; it's your free will. How are you programmed? You must become consciously aware of your knowing, your thoughts, your choices, and your actions. If you are not, you will continue to live in an unconscious, routine, fear-based state of thinking.

Earlier, I mentioned becoming the hamster on the wheel. The hamster runs faster and faster and never goes anywhere. Eventually, the hamster runs until he is exhausted or falls over. What has he accomplished? Nothing! So often, we are like the hamster on the wheel. We run faster and faster to obtain more and more struggle, exhaust ourselves mentally, physically, emotionally, and never go anywhere. We're always striving and never arriving. Then maybe one day, we wake up, refuse to hit the snooze button again, and begin to ask questions: Why am I choosing this way of living? Is there a better way? Otherwise, we end up like the hamster, and we run until we fall from the wheel with exhaustion, wasting a life in which we never seemed to fulfill our purpose. Again, this is your choice, your free will. The only person on the wheel is you. The only person to choose to stay in fear and struggle is you. The only person to make the choice for significant change and to get off the wheel is you. You must stop pointing the finger, blaming others or events, and stop sabotaging yourself by making excuses for your life.

The only guaranteed time we have is right now, and the time you have to change is right now. You didn't get here over night, and it will take commitment, effort, and practice to make a significant change. The good news is your life can change and improve if you have faith and commitment, along with a willingness to accept responsibility for your choices and surrender your fear, pain, and struggle to God. You can acknowledge your past; learn from it and begin to understand how your choices led you to this point. You can redefine the objective for your résumé. If you are still on the hamster wheel, you can make a conscious choice to recognize it right now along with the conscious decision to get off. At this point, you can open yourself up to make more conscious internal, knowing choices that lead to freedom, peace, love, and awareness. Throughout our day, we can choose to respond with love, peace, and kindness, or we can choose to respond with anger, hate, and judgment. When you learn to recognize these events and how you can respond to them, you will be on the path to open yourself up to more of the same of your own choosing.

Recognize and define your objective for your life—what do you want to do? Recognize how you are programmed—is it positive in, positive out? Or is it garbage in, garbage out? Are you the hamster on the wheel? If so, are you ready to get off the wheel? Are your choices leading you to rewards or consequences? You have been given free will. What are you doing with it?

Self-Reflection

(This space is provided for you to reflect on
how you can apply what you've read.)

CHAPTER 5

Energy

WE ARE NOW TO THE point of understanding that everything is composed of energy. *Webster's American Dictionary* defines energy as "... the power that is waiting and can be used. [It is] the power of certain forces in nature to do work. Power or strength suggests the ability to act upon something or to hold out or last. Power is a general word used to mean the ability to do something either in a physical way or with the mind." For your résumé, energy will be a part of your educational experience to help you better understand and use what you have learned.

Everything we are and everything we create is composed of energy. It is a vibrational and physical manifestation of creation. Everything you see around you and have obtained on the physical realm has been created by an idea, dream, or inspiration and has developed into the physical form for you to see, hear, touch, taste, or use. This energy that has manifested into the physical form also includes you and your family and friends. It includes the house you occupy, the car you drive, the food you eat, and the clothes you wear. Everything and everyone is made up of energy. Everything and everyone has a purpose and is here for a purpose.

Once you become more consciously aware and recognize these key points, you can begin the process of gratitude for who you are and for the actual power and strength you have been given. When you understand that you have been given everything you need for this life, you can refocus your life and your thought process. Everything you have encountered in your school of life has brought you to here and now. The experiences you have encountered during your journey are a part of your résumé's life education. You should begin the process of identifying what these events mean for you. You should also gain a better understanding of who you really are. The question is, what will you do with your life's education? How have you handled or dealt with the events in your life? Remember that everything is energy and a vibrational manifestation of your thoughts, creation, and ideas.

If you are always worried about what you want and what you don't have, you will continue to receive more of the same. If you are constantly in a state of struggle and want, you will remain in that state of struggle and want. If something wonderful happens in your life, and you are constantly worried that it will be taken away or questioning what you did to deserve it, you have wasted your time and energy in a state of fear and worry instead of happiness and gratitude. If you're always seeing the glass half-empty or waiting for the other shoe to drop, then rest assured, that thinking will manifest. This is your energy and how you are choosing to use it.

You must allow for positive opportunities and gifts to enter your life and maintain a sense of appreciation and gratitude for them. Energy is always moving and vibrating. Appreciate and be grateful for what you have now; otherwise, you can use your energy in a state of fearful thoughts, such as not deserving a gift or waiting for it to be lost or taken away. Energy is always moving and flowing, and we cannot control energy any more than if we try to feel, grab, or hold on to electricity. You have to be grateful and nurture what you have at the time you have it—in the now. Why? Because now is all you have and all you will ever have. Appreciate and make the best use of your energy right here and now. Be grateful today because no one knows what tomorrow will bring. Always know and believe that God will bring you what you need, right on time and when you need it. It may come wrapped as a miracle and a gift, or it may come wrapped as a lesson you are to learn and grow from.

We are all here on our own journey to grow and learn. We are here to become the best we can be, to create, to help, and to teach or to learn from others along the way. This is energy, and this is growth, power, and strength. It is our knowing and our truth. Remember—if God brings it to you, then you need to learn from it and be grateful for it since these are your educational lessons in your résumé of life. These lessons help you understand how you arrived at where you are in your life—here and now.

Oftentimes, many of us allow our energy to get tied up into our coping mechanisms. We all have coping mechanisms that we use during stressful, fearful, or painful situations in our life. Here is a list of some common coping mechanisms:

- eating
- anger
- blaming
- shutting down
- running and hiding
- drugs
- alcohol
- sex
- searching for other people or other things to make us feel better
- overspending
- excessive worry

Identify and recognize your coping mechanism(s) and ask yourself this question: is my coping mechanism really working for me? My guess is that it really is not.

Most of our coping mechanisms usually lead to more guilt, shame, or pain that we inflict upon others and ourselves. For example, if you eat to cope, you probably have some guilt or shame after you eat, and your weight and health may likely be an issue. Did it remove the stress, anxiety, or fear that caused this coping mechanism to kick in? On the other hand, did it simply create more anxiety, shame, guilt, or fear? Here is another example. If you turn to drugs or alcohol, neither allows you to deal with the situation. If using drugs or alcohol is your way of coping, it may lead to poor health, hangovers, or you may even hurt or kill someone else. Later, you may find yourself apologizing for what you did while you were not in your "right" mind, and you may have even caused more chaos and damage. This coping mechanism will only feed your addiction, and it will only provide a momentary escape from the actual situation. Did it remove the painful, stressful event that led you to drink alcohol or use drugs to cope? Or did it cause further damage and pile more problems on the initial issue at hand?

We have continued to seek things outside of ourselves to cope or to self-medicate. We have used them in an attempt to feel better. However, these physical things are only a temporary fix; they will never last. When do we realize that we have everything we need inside of us? Our spirit, our knowing, has always been there and will always be there. How many times do we push our snooze button on our alarm clock before we realize that we have to listen to our spiritual selves, have faith in our spiritual selves, and build our spiritual muscles? Again, you are made up of energy, so how are you using it? Are you using your energy as a negative, external escape from the fear, anxiety, or worry? If so, how is that working for you?

As you may recall from my life's résumé, I spent a lot of time running from fear of rejection. My coping mechanism was to run and hide in fear. When I was younger, I was involved in sports and exercise and was in good physical shape. I had many friends and felt confident and happy with my life. After I went through the pain and loss of my job, community, and friends and experienced so much hurt and rejection, I turned to food to self-medicate. I put on a lot of weight, and my appearance, health, and self-confidence began to decline. I continued to search for love and acceptance from others, only to remain in a continuous cycle of feeling like I was not good enough. I was afraid of my truth. I didn't know who I was. I always worried about what others thought of me. I was seeking and searching for something or someone outside of myself to accept me or to help me feel better about myself.

For years, I ran and carried that fear and pain with me because I was afraid of what others would think or how I would be treated. It kept me in a position of struggle, distrust, and pain. It also allowed me to keep my distance from others and to hide behind the façade of the weight. What I didn't realize was that if I didn't accept myself, how could anyone else? I tried to overcompensate in my job performance and my friendships, searching for any type of acceptance. I looked for things and people outside of myself, searching for that feeling of love and belonging. Eating became a momentary comfort. It was something to pass the time but only for the minutes it took to eat, and then that comfort was gone, and guilt quickly set in. This took a tremendous amount of negative energy and work on my part, and I still never really felt whole and accepted. Because of the fear and pain I had experienced, I continued to feed my negative side. I carried a lot of anger, hurt, distrust, and pain over many years. I ran from one thing to another, always in search of happiness. It was exhausting, and I spent my energy going nowhere and inflicting pain upon myself. I didn't believe in myself; therefore, I could not listen to, learn from, and build my spiritual muscle from within. I kept pushing my snooze button.

Now, I have come to recognize I was using my energy in a negative way. I was the hamster on the wheel, always running and never going anywhere. I didn't love and accept myself; therefore, I became my own self-fulfilling prophecy—complete with fear, rejection, and pain.

Ask yourself, how am I using my energy? Am I using my energy positively and faithfully or is my energy feeding the negative side of me? What am I to learn from my experiences throughout my life's journey? Am I trying to hold on to past events that caused me pain or trying to control outcomes? Instead of remaining in the thinking that "I'm not good enough" or "I don't deserve better," what would it feel like if you actually stated, felt, and believed that you were good enough and did deserve better?

Review your résumé and the events, people, and places you have encountered along your journey. Begin to ask about which events you may have continued to repeat in various forms. What was I to learn from these life lessons? How can I grow from them instead of holding on to anger, blame, or judgment? No one has done anything to you; they have been in your life to help you or for you to help them to grow and gain a better awareness and strength of self.

We must learn from these lessons and ask the hard questions:

- What was this experience here to teach me?
- How can I grow from it?
- What am I doing with my energy that keeps me in the same patterns that cause me fear, pain, anger, and struggle?
- What are my coping mechanisms?
- Do my coping mechanisms actually help me or do they perpetuate more of the same?

When you look at it from a conscious, open, and positive perspective and with a willingness to seek the truth about yourself, you will change your thought process. Your life will change, and you will become consciously aware of who you are and begin to define your truth, your love, and your purpose. Your energy will move in a more positive realm as you consciously become more in tune and aware that your thoughts are energy that manifest your educational experiences into your physical world. Your world will become more peaceful, and you may find you have more energy to do the things you love.

What you put out into the world will come back to you multiplied. We fall into habits of thinking in certain ways, and that can either be our greatest gift or our biggest downfall. So, as the old saying goes, "some habits die hard, and some habits are made to be broken." Your thoughts and choices define you, and you will reap what you sow. This is energy, and you can choose to have your energy work for you or against you. When a stressful situation arises, here are four steps to help your energy work for you:

1. Recognize your energy and what you are feeling.
2. Allow energy to flow through you. Do not try to grasp or hold on to it or act out in a negative, angry way.
3. Remove yourself from the negative situation until it can be dealt with in a more positive manner.
4. Surrender it to a higher power.

Energy, like electricity, cannot be grasped or contained, and it works on a positive and negative pole. Just as electricity works on a positive and negative pole, you too are made up of both positive and negative, with yin and yang or light and dark. You are made up of both positive and negative, and you encounter both throughout your journey. It's how quickly you can identify it and how you use it that will make the difference.

Let's look at these two examples. First, one of the strongest forms of energy is the ocean. The ocean is a form of energy that we can actually feel, see, hear, taste, and touch. It is a massive, powerful energy source that must be respected. We use the ocean for our vacation destinations to relax and unwind. It can provide a sense of healing, peace, and calmness for us. The ocean sustains life and provides us with food, and even provides medical and healing benefits. The ocean is a powerful energy source that is constantly moving and flowing. You cannot grasp, hold on to, or control this powerful energy source. The energy and power of the ocean must be respected, or it can hurt you or even take your life.

The ocean consists of ebb and flow—as the tide comes in, the tide goes out. If you think about it, the ocean is much like our own lives; we too have ebbs and flows. If we encounter an ebb in our life, we must recognize it as such, learn from it, believe that it will pass, and know the flow will always return. How quickly we recognize the ebb and how we deal with it is what makes the difference. We will also have flow in our life. This is a time to be grateful, rather than a time of fear and worry about how long will it last or when it will be taken away. Again, how quickly we recognize the flow and how we deal with it makes the difference.

Energy must flow. It cannot be controlled, held on to, or maintained no more than you can control, hold on to, or maintain electricity or the ocean. As we refer to ebb and flow with the ocean, we use positive and negative current with electricity. All forms of energy must be allowed to flow.

Second, electricity, like the ocean, is a powerful energy source that we use daily in our lives, and it too must be respected; otherwise, it can hurt you or kill you. Just as we use the ocean as an energy source, we also use electricity as a heating and cooling source, and as a charging source for our cars, our electronics, and so on.

I've used these analogies of electricity and the ocean to help you become more consciously aware of just how powerful energy is and to help you understand that everything is made up of energy. You too are made up of energy, and I hope you have become more aware of just how powerful you are. You see, energy is ageless, timeless, and is not gender specific. It is the core—the essence—of who you are and the power you have within. You can use your energy in a positive way and provide love, healing, and strength to yourself and others. On the other hand, you can use your energy in a negative, hateful, judgmental way and disrespect the truth of who you are and the truth of others. If you choose to feed your negative side, then it can be detrimental to you, your health, and to others. Again, you are energy. Your thoughts are energy. Your thoughts create the world you live in. You need to become consciously aware and observant that everything around you and within in you is energy and seek a better understanding of how it flows and how you are using it.

If you build your energy upon your love, goodness, light, and strength, then your anger, resentments, and weaknesses will lessen. If you build your positive side, then the negative side will lessen. As you know, the darkness dissipates when you shine a light on it. You have the choice (free will) to recognize, feed, nurture, and grow your positive, love, goodness, light, and strength, or you can feed the negative side by continuing to complain about your problems, self-medicate, worry about what you don't have or deserve, along with feeding your coping skills and weaknesses. With this choice, you will continue to expend your energy in an exhaustive manner, only to remain in your own internal fear and struggle.

A father was teaching his son a valuable lesson one day by explaining that we had two wolves battling inside of us. One wolf was good—representing love, joy, peace, truth, strength, light, and kindness. The other wolf was bad—representing fear, judgment, darkness, anger, resentment, and lies. The son asked, "Father, which wolf wins the battle?" The father replied, "The one that you feed!"

Which wolf do you choose to feed?

SELF-REFLECTION

(This space is provided for you to reflect on
how you can apply what you've read.)

CHAPTER 6

Taking Care of You

In taking care of you, your résumé should include your skills and abilities. Whether you have recognized them or not, you have been provided with inherent skills and abilities. You are here to create, to help, to teach, to learn, and to experience this physical realm called life. You have been provided with your own personal set of skills and abilities. They were designed to make your life journey a better experience for you and for others. You are here to fulfill your purpose and to experience joy, love, peace, and gratitude. More importantly, you are here to share that with all who you encounter along your path. People, events, and things happen throughout our journeys, and how we create, respond, and receive these gifts is totally up to us. Make a list of your skills and abilities and those things that feed your passion. Make a list of things in your life you are grateful for, and begin to add new ideas to your list and carry it with you throughout your day.

Life provides us gifts. For example, a new and exciting relationship, a promotion at work, a wonderful trip, a child, a new pet, a new friend, and so on. You should always feel gratitude for the people, places, or things you receive and never take them for granted. Life also provides us with difficult lessons, whether it is a loss of a loved one, a pet, a job, a home, and so on. Even in these difficult times, we should be grateful for the lessons and learn from them. We should also find a way to carry those gifts and lessons in our hearts so we may continue to learn and to grow from them. A loss of a relationship or a loss because of death can cause us significant pain; we should allow ourselves time to grieve this loss. We should check our energy and take the time to grieve. On the other hand, we cannot remain indefinitely in that loss and grief, or it will cause stagnation and stunt our growth. Honor those who have gone on not by continuing to remain in grief but by using what they gave you. Honor them by recognizing what they taught you and share those gifts with others. Make their journey worthwhile by remembering them in love. Allow the gifts they provided to you to come through you and be grateful for what they accomplished and taught in their lives. Learn to pay it forward and share that love and growth.

You also cannot control people, events, or things. Day turns to night, and night turns to day. The sun comes up, and then the moon and stars. Storms come, and then there is a calm, a freshness, and sometimes even a rainbow! We all experience seasons throughout the year—spring, summer, fall, and winter. People are born; they grow; they age; and they pass. Life is just this way—light and dark, clear skies and storms, seasons and change. Occasionally, we even encounter a few rainbows along our journeys! In comparison, we all have our seasons of life. While we are here, we have the opportunity to create a better place, to enhance our skills and abilities, and to make a difference.

It is never too late to change and to make a difference. If you're having thoughts like "I'm too old," or "I'm too fat," or "I'm too tired," or too whatever, then start right now to change your energy by releasing those ego-based, negative thoughts and change them to *I can, I will, and I am.* Then you do it! Tell yourself right now that you love yourself and that you are special. Begin to believe in you, believe in your skills, and believe in your abilities. You are a part of God and know that you recognize and glorify God when you do this. Begin to know this, practice it, and believe it in your heart. Do not allow anyone to make you feel less than who you really are. Know here and now that you are a glorified manifestation of God. You are just as special and important as the next person. This belief and this practice will put you on the path to taking care of you. It is up to you to recognize, realize, understand, believe, and accept this, for it is truth, and it is love.

The Power of Affirmations

Affirmations become a valuable key at this point. You must verbalize and begin to *believe* that you are special! You are not an accident. You are here for a purpose, and you must believe in you. True affirmations begin with two words: *I am.* Think, verbalize, and believe in your affirmations. Affirm that: *I am* ... love, light, abundance, success, truth, healthy, grateful, whatever the case may be. You can do this as you exercise, as you drive to and from work, when you wake up, before you go to bed, any time of the day or night. Begin teaching affirmations to your children. Play games to help them find positive words to describe themselves. This is a wonderful use of your time and energy. As you use your affirmations, you will become more consciously aware of yourself and your surroundings. Have faith and love yourself. Be grateful for who you are.

Affirmations are the steps toward strengthening your spirit and building your spiritual muscle. It is not about how much physical wealth you have, the car you drive, how tall, short, fat, thin or popular you are. These are outside, physical things. It is about who you are inside and what you are here to do. If you begin to feel and believe you are beautiful on the inside, you will find yourself changing the way you treat yourself and the way you treat others. You will also see others responding to you in a more positive way.

Begin the process of taking care of you, of strengthening your Spirit, and let your light shine! All things happen right on time, and everything happens at the right time for the right reason. Take now todo something positive for yourself and for someone else. Take now to be positive, creative and grateful. Take now to wake up to your purpose and your potential. Take now to identify your innate skills and abilities. You arrived with these skills and abilities; are you using them? Have you even recognized them? Now is the only time we ever truly have. Now is the time we have to make a positive difference in our own lives and in the lives of others.

You must become loving, kind, peaceful, and comfortable on the inside before you can have these things on the outside. So, we are back to what you think about expands. Go within and find your truth, your love, your peace, and your gratitude. Once you begin to do this, practice this, allow for this, and believe this, then you will begin to manifest it in the physical realm, and your life will begin to improve. I cannot express enough how powerful your thoughts are and how powerful and special you are. You can be all you can imagine and more if you believe in yourself. Get out of your own way and out of your *ego* mind that feeds you with negativity and criticism. Remember—your ego mind wants to keep you in a state of fear, anger, judgment, worry, and anxiety. Go within to find your spirit (knowing) and begin to allow for the goodness, love, and the peace that is inside of you to grow and to expand. Allow your spirit to feed your mind instead of the outside influences. Find your true self, the one that is inside of you, the one that has been here since you arrived and will always be here with you.

If you are reading this book, then the right thing is happening at the right time. Now you can allow your truth to be born, to come to light, to grow and to begin to expand into the wonderful gift and positive manifestation of who you truly are. It's time to stop searching for things outside of yourself in the vain attempt to find love, peace, truth, happiness, and acceptance. Your true happiness and peace comes from within. If the outside things have not worked for you or brought you lasting joy, then maybe it's time to try a different route. The route to true lasting peace, freedom, love, and light is the route that you already possess within, not to be found without. Confucius said, "A journey of a thousand miles begins with a single step." Your new journey has begun.

The Power of Meditation

To begin improving on your skills and abilities, it is wise to find some time in your day to meditate. This will create peace and balance in your life. Take a moment to turn off the outside noise, such as television, radio, cell phone, and so on. Find a place of quiet, peace, and stillness so that you can relax and go within. Let go of worries and ask for peace. Listen to your breathing and find the peace and stillness you have within you. Stop your ego and negative thoughts and just allow yourself to be in a quiet, peaceful place. Meditation is something anyone can do at any moment. It is most important to make time for meditation. Meditation can become the most important and best use of your time and energy in your life. It is a time to go within, to listen to your inner voice, your God self. It is the time to find balance, relaxation, creativity, and peace. It is within that you will find your true answers; however, you must be willing to ask, then be patient and listen.

Meditation takes practice and commitment. Once you begin to

meditate regularly, even if you simply begin with ten or fifteen minutes, you will find yourself growing and becoming stronger every day. Believe in yourself; take this opportunity to grow from within yourself. This is your life and your journey, and you cannot truly love or be capable of receiving love if you do not build love within yourself. Meditation is a time for listening and refueling, which will allow you to grow and become who you are meant to be and to realize your life's purpose. It is a time to open up, to give and to receive. This is the opportunity to find and realize the truth of who you are.

I stated that this was a guide for becoming consciously aware through spirit, mind, and body. If you go within to find, recognize, and get to know spirit (truth, guidance, and purpose), then mind (ego, thoughts) and body (physical body, actions) will follow. When you trust and allow for spirit to guide you, your mind and actions will become kinder, peaceful, and loving.

You must be clear about what you want but also know that you will receive what you need. This also becomes a practice in patience and in faith. If it is peace you want, then go within to find peace. When you think and feel peace, your life will become more peaceful. A side benefit is you may find things are done more easily, with far less effort and in far less time. Be open and allow these things to happen and then recognize and be grateful when they come. If it is love you want, then go within and find the love for yourself. Practice, recognize, feel, and have love for yourself. Affirm: "I am love; I am loving; I am loved." You will become loving and be able to give love (without conditions), and it will be multiplied back to you. To have what you want, you must become what you want. It is then you will become more conscious of the gifts you receive. Become a vessel of peace, love, generosity, and gratitude.

If it's money you want, then thinking in terms of never having enough will bring more of the same, and that is never enough! Clarify and focus on already having enough and be grateful for what you already have. If you are caught in the trap of always wanting more, spending more, and constantly struggling to obtain more, then that is what you will continue to have. Furthermore, you must practice gratitude for what you have already received. If you do not appreciate and care for what you have obtained, then what makes you think you deserve more? God will always provide for you what you need. It is ultimately your choice and responsibility for what you do with it.

The Process of Taking Care of You

Begin the process of taking care of you. How? Let go of negativity and recognize and build your inherent skills and abilities. Remember no one can do it for you. We all have our journeys or our paths to walk. While we can share in another's journey, we cannot walk in another's journey. Simply put, you cannot walk in someone else's shoes! Just as you have your choices and experiences, so do others. You cannot fix, judge, or control others, and trying to do so only leads you astray and away from your true self. If you continue to focus on everyone else, then you cannot truly focus on yourself. You must be willing to put forth the effort to believe in and to work on you. It's time to stop judging and blaming others for what they have or for what they do. It is a waste of your energy and only distracts you from your own journey. Deal with yourself and take care of you. If you do not take care of you, then how can you truly teach and help others? If you do not know your truth or understand your skills and abilities, then how do you propose to share yourself with others or to create and find your purpose? If you are not in a place of peace and love, then how do you propose to expand and create a better world for yourself and for those around you? Again, my gentle reminder:

- Recognize, feel, believe, allow, and be grateful for the gifts you have already been given.
- Recognize and list your skills and abilities.
- Recite, practice, believe, and feel your affirmations.

What are you passionate about? What stirs your creativity? Take a few moments each day and find a quiet place to go within and meditate. This is taking care of you, and if you practice these things daily, you will enhance your spirit and feel it growing stronger. Your internal light will become brighter as you become more empowered and enlightened. You will start to feel your life and your world change, grow, and improve.

Affirmations Lead to Transformation

(This space is provided for you to write your own affirmations.)

CHAPTER 7

Sow a Seed

I WORKED MANY YEARS IN inpatient psychiatric treatment, which was a job filled with depression, anger, hurt, drug abuse, sex abuse, hatred, distrust, and various psychiatric issues. It was a difficult job, and I worked very hard to establish trusting relationships with the patients. I wanted to help them establish a more peaceful and productive way of living than what they were accustomed to experiencing.

I am reminded of a thirteen-year-old patient, a beautiful little girl who was placed in the hospital for severe depression and suicide attempts. She had been abused, neglected, and abandoned by her family. All she wanted was to be loved and accepted. While she was in our care, she left the group session to go to the bathroom and attempted to hang herself in the closet. I was the first person on the scene and the one to untie the sheet and get her down. I had only been working inpatient treatment for a few months and had never experienced such an event in my life. It made me question so many things.

This poor child was instilled with fear, rejection, and depression. It was a devastating event for both her and for me. We ended up working through some of her fears and trust issues, and she began to gain a feeling of self-worth. Because I was the one to find and help her, she came to trust me more than any of the other staff. She began to feel as though someone cared. We ended up finding family members who were willing to work with her, to love her, and to provide a loving, accepting home. A year later, I heard from her, and she was beginning to grow and blossom. I would like to believe I helped her, but deep down, I know she helped me too.

The success rate is very low, and when a patient was successful, it made it all worthwhile. We were constantly challenged to find ways to get the patient to open up and to trust. Even though there were many sad stories and cases that most people could never stand to hear, I still remained constant and worked to try to help every patient in my care. In virtually every case, they only wanted to be loved and accepted and to have someone to trust and believe in. Unfortunately, many of them only experienced fear, pain, rejection, and abuse throughout their lives.

Years later, I changed jobs and ended up working in the sales and customer service industry. It too is a process of building positive relationships, establishing trust, and helping the client to see the value in what I'm providing or attempting to sell. I remember when I first began, I had gone into a client's office to introduce myself, and as soon as I told them who I was and the company I worked for, they literally threw unpaid bills at me. They had not seen a service rep for a long time and were disgusted and ready to quit. I explained that I was new to the company and asked for an opportunity to try to resolve their issues. I listened to what they had to say and told them I would follow up with them within the next two days. As promised, I returned within two days with resolutions for their issues. My follow-up and effort to establish trust is what salvaged that account, and I began to establish rapport as their representative.

The similarity of both jobs is that the client also needed to be able to establish trust, to feel heard or accepted, and to recognize that I cared and did what I said I would do. Over the years, that same client has become one of my most cherished and valued customers. The position gave me the opportunity to establish trust and rapport with the client in an effort to resolve their issue with a positive outcome. Sometimes I had to be creative and think outside the box in an effort to resolve certain issues. Although there were times that I had to admit defeat and could not resolve an issue, it still did not deter me from continuing to move on to the next issue and resolve it.

For me, both industries consisted of establishing and building trusting relationships, helping resolve issues, and working to create a better and acceptable situation for others and myself. My purpose was to gain a better awareness of my true self and to identify and enhance my skills and abilities. I've come to recognize that it's all about giving and helping others. I love helping others to resolve issues and gain a better awareness of themselves. It's an act of sowing seeds of faith, positivity, truth, and enlightenment. Both industries, although on opposite ends of the spectrum, allowed me to be creative, to grow, and to help others to grow. When you carry the thought of "How can I help?" and you follow through to help others, this becomes the basis for the seeds you sow. These seeds will always help you and others to grow and prosper.

As I recognized some of my unique skills and abilities, I realized I still struggled with worrying about others' opinions. So many of us think we have to be someone or something that we are not. We've been told that we should be like or act like someone else to be successful or happy. Many of us want or envy what someone else has, whether it is their money, prestige, position, home, family, and so on. We may even hide behind a mask of trying to be something or someone we are not in an effort to impress or to gain acceptance or attention from others. We allow others to tell us what we should do, how we should be, or that we should act a certain way. The truth is we are all special, and we are all here to recognize and fulfill our own unique purposes while on our journeys.

If any of these statements resonated with you, then you may have yet to identify or may have begun to recognize or use your own unique skills and abilities. We are not here to mimic others or to envy what others may have already obtained on their journey. We need to become all we are meant to be in our own unique way in whatever capacity or form that may take. If we continue to focus all our energy wanting what someone else has, judging how someone else is living, or listening to outside negative influences, then we are diminishing our own truth and purpose and remaining on the road of striving and never arriving. We are wasting our own skills and abilities and diminishing the truth of who we are and what we are meant to do in our own lives.

We are here to find, create, experience, and share our own positive light, love, and truth and to make our own stamp or statement on this journey. Do not waste any more of your precious energy and time focusing on what others have, how they should live, or what others think. Every one of us has our own journey and path to walk and to excel at. If we choose to continue to try to go down someone else's path, then we will never fulfill our own true destiny. We are all connected; we are all a part of the whole, and if we truly love ourselves and truly listen to our spirit to guide us, then we will always be in a true state of love, light, giving, receiving, and being.

During our lifetime, we get caught up in what others think we should do or be and lose sight of who we truly are. Finding, believing, and walking in your own truth is how you will find and become all you are meant to be. If you begin to recognize and practice this, your life will become more peaceful and positive. You will acquire a knowing that you are right where you need to be, and you will begin to have faith that everything is unfolding just how it should. You will begin to grow, create, and change in a more positive light. You can become who you are meant to be—a more positive, loving, light-filled reflection of God. This is what God wants for you! You will recognize and be grateful for the little things and the gifts that come into your life. You will gain an appreciation for who you are and all that you have begun to manifest in your spiritual and physical world. Your life should become more peaceful and positive. The things that used to make you angry or stressed should not be so overwhelming anymore. You can learn to stop the negativity in its tracks when you feel it begin to arise. You will begin to make time for you and for others with less worry, anxiety, and struggle.

When you stop letting outside worries of people and things get in the way of the time you spend actually enjoying and being grateful for who you are and what you have received, you will begin to have more peace, joy, and wisdom. This is when you stop blaming, judging, or controlling others. This is when you stop using these things as excuses for why you can't enjoy or appreciate all you have in your life. It is time to get out of your own way, let go of the façade, and begin to recognize your truth and your spirit. No one put you in this position, only you. No one can get you in a better position, only you. You've always had the choice (free will) to decide how you think, speak, and act. You are the one to create the world you are living in.

It is time to come to the realization that the important things in life are those of love, light, peace, joy, truth, faith, and wisdom. It is a way of being and knowing that will always provide more of what you need. It is a peace and a truth that cannot be bought or forced. It is a gift of giving and receiving from your true self and the gift you share with others. This is who you truly are. We should never stop learning and creating, for if we do, we become stagnant and unhealthy. We must let go of envy, pain, and struggle and allow for giving and receiving of good in our life. Be grateful for the little things, the quality time you spend with family, friends, pets, or self. Be grateful for the time you spend doing self-reflection and listening to Spirit in meditation. These things do not cost money and should not be a struggle. It is your choice to practice and begin to live this way or to stay where you are.

However, if you are not happy where you are, then maybe it's time to try an alternative route. Again, this is your free will, and you can push aside your skills and abilities, or you can recognize and begin to enhance them. In fact, your skills and abilities can bring you more of who you are as a vessel of love, joy, light, truth, wisdom, and peace. These are the things we are here to do: to create, to teach, to learn, to grow, to help, and to provide. If you have spent your energy and time in fear, worry, and struggle over what others have, how others live their lives, or what others may think about you, you have likely continued down that very same road, repeatedly. Is it working for you? Have the outcomes brought you any peace, truth, or joy? Have your outcomes continued to provide you with more fear, worry, struggle, or maybe even lost relationships? Are you continuing to experience events that lead to same or similar outcomes? Do you have an appreciation for yourself and others? Do you have an appreciation or feel joy for who you are and what you are doing in your life? Do you recognize and appreciate the little things in life? What type of seeds are you sowing?

We have allowed ourselves to get caught up in the rat race of always striving and never arriving. We have lost sight of the truly important things in life. Can you identify your skills and abilities in your physical job? Are you able to identify your skills and abilities for your life's purpose? Are there any comparisons in your physical jobs that allow you to realize your spiritual purpose?

By understanding the common element in my physical jobs, I have realized my purpose is to give myself in faith, hope, strength, love, peace, and truth and to help others have a more productive and positive outcome. I ask myself the question, "How can I help?" This is also the basis for this book. It has been written to sow a seed of faith and thought for you and to help you to create, to grow, to find the truth of who you are, and to find your love and acceptance within. I hope it will help you to look at things with a different perspective and become more consciously aware of your spirit, mind, and body. If you begin to recognize and be grateful for the little things, and begin to find joy and gratitude throughout your day, you will begin to find that the little nuances in life don't become bigger problems. Moreover, the bigger problems may begin to dissolve, magically and miraculously. If you sow seeds of fear, anger, worry, and judgment, then that is what you will grow.

If you sow seeds of love, peace, light, and gratitude, then that is what you will grow. You must recognize the types of seeds you are sowing, as you can't plant grass and expect to see a rose garden. Darkness dissipates when light is shone upon it. The overwhelming issues you allow to grow are compared to the darkness that disappears when light is shone upon it. If you sow seeds of love and light, then the huge, fear-based, overwhelming issues begin to lose their power over you.

How do you eat an elephant? The answer is one bite at a time! Do something today to find and give goodness, love, and light to yourself and to others. Be grateful for doing all you can do in any given day. Ask yourself, "How can I help?" Become consciously aware and grateful for the little things that come along in your day. Take a moment before you go to bed and recognize the little things from your day that you are grateful for. Think, verbalize, and feel gratitude for your day. Take a break from that busy project and spend some quality time throwing a ball in the yard with your child. Attend an event that your child or partner is in. Show genuine interest in someone else, whether it is a family member, a friend, or a stranger. Give a smile and a hello to the stranger you pass on the street or in a store. Slow down and hold a door open for others. Smile and say thank you (show gratitude) if someone opens a door for you. Be grateful for those little things you've been ignoring throughout your day and your life. Be kind, generous, giving, and grateful to everyone you meet, including the person at the drive-through window or checkout counter. Be grateful in your giving and in your receiving. If someone has been in your thoughts, pick up the phone and give them a call. There is a reason they are in your thoughts.

This is your spirit speaking to you, and you need to listen. Become more consciously aware of your thoughts and actions throughout your day.

Once you begin to practice this, you will see your life and health improve and change. Come to believe and know that there is a reason for everything. Love and patience are virtues; practicing them in everything and with everyone you encounter on a daily basis in your journey will only serve to benefit you and those around you. What you give, you shall receive multiplied. These are just some of your skills and abilities that you can begin to recognize, enhance, and grow. What types of seed(s) will you sow today?

SELF-REFLECTION

(This space is provided for you to reflect on
how you can apply what you've read.)

CHAPTER 8

Balance

YOU CAN BEGIN TO FIND balance in your life and stay out of the extremes by going to your center or your Source. You cannot find balance if you do not understand what balance is. *Webster's Dictionary* defines *balance* three ways:

1) Equality in amount, weight, value, or importance between two things or the parts of a single thing
2) The ability to keep one's body steady without falling
3) A person's normal, steady state of mind

The third definition better describes the balance we must focus on—our state of mind. While still gaining an understanding of your innate skills and abilities, you should recognize that we often allow outside events or people to take us to one extreme or the other. In other words, we are out of balance. Once you begin to recognize these events for what they are, you can make the choice to go to the extreme of negativity and anger, or you can make the choice to remain in balance. You can do this in a myriad of ways, but first you must begin to recognize it when it comes. If you are beginning to recognize and use your innate skills and abilities, they will become stronger and more effective for you when stressful, negative situations arise.

Once you identify a stressful event has just taken place or something was said that made you angry, you must recognize it before you allow it to take you to the point of extreme anger, worry, or agitation. You possess the skills and abilities to find your balance, and you must use them to do it. Before you speak or act out or send that negative, retaliating email or text, you need to take a moment and find your balance. Recognize immediately when you are allowing an outside event, person, place, or thing to take you out of your center.

Allow your skills to help you through these stressful situations. Tests will come, and it is up to you whether you pass or fail. Think before you speak or act in a negative, judgmental, angry manner. Go within, find your Source, and ask for peace and answers. You may need to take some deep breaths, or you may need to remove yourself from the situation, count to one hundred, and so on.

Balance and Anger

There are numerous choices you can make when a negative situation arises, but the one choice you do not want to make is to retaliate in anger. Anger is a negative energy force that only leads to counterforce, further escalation, retaliation, and regrets. Nothing gets solved in the heat of the moment or in the heat of anger and violence. It only multiplies with more anger, more arguments, and more violence. Again, if you think it and act in accordance with it, you will receive it. If you take some time to regain your composure or your balance, more will be resolved with less conflict. Negativity and conflict are not a competition of who wins or loses. There are no winners in conflict, only casualties.

Work to remain within your balance or your Source, and remember it is here where you will find peace, answers, and enlightenment. You will resolve more conflict in a peaceful, positive manner without further violence and regrets. As you begin to practice this, you will improve your overall health. If you choose to remain in a constant state of worry, struggle, and agitation, it will change your body's biochemistry and will manifest into physical health issues.

Again, what you think about expands into the physical realm.

The Grandfather Clock

As I have come to find my balance and been honest with myself, I have come to recognize that many of us live in extremes. We operate on one end of the scale or the other. Some of us vacillate between both extremes. I am reminded of our antique grandfather clock that my parents brought back from Germany while they were stationed there in the military. I grew up with that clock, listening to the bongs during the night that would occur on the hour and half hour. It would provide me with comfort to know what time it was and that everything was okay. I would hear my mother wind it every morning, and I knew she would be coming to my room to wake me up for school. The grandfather clock was a centerpiece of our house and had a pendulum that swung from one side to the other.

Now that I am older, I recognize that as I grew up listening and watching the pendulum on the clock, many of us live our lives in much the same way. We seem to vacillate from one side to the other in extremes. However, as the pendulum swings from one side to the other, it briefly passes through its center but does not remain there. To stop the clock, the pendulum must rest in the center and not swing. When the pendulum is centered and at rest, everything on the clock becomes quiet and peaceful, and there is no swinging, chaos, or ticking. When negativity begins to arise, you must center yourself and stop your clock; slow things down to a restful, peaceful, balance and calmness within. Do not *allow* other people or events to take you out of your balance.

The only one who can find your balance is you. The only one who can remove yourself from your balance is you. No one did it to you; you allowed it to happen. When you allow people or events to take you out of your balance, you have given them your power and your strength. It is your responsibility to remain in your balance and to operate within it. If you feel you are being pulled out of balance, then it is your responsibility to recognize it and go back to it. Remember that when your energy is centered in your core—your balance—this is when you are the strongest and most powerful. This is a difficult lesson and thing to do, but it can be done, and you can do it. Like the pendulum on that old grandfather clock, you must be centered to remain restful, peaceful, and balanced.

Avoid Extremes

You must find your balance, recognize it, work with it, and allow yourself to recognize people and events that you allow to take you out of your balance. I have provided an example diagram of identifiable extreme words along with identifiable balance words. I hope you will recognize where you are on the scale. You may identify with some of these words or be reminded of others not listed here.

Ask yourself if you operate predominantly in one extreme or the other. Do you vacillate between both extremes? If you vacillate, just as the pendulum on the clock, you must pass through your balance to get to extremes. Do you recognize your balance while you pass through it or do you just swing from one extreme to the other and never take a moment to find your balance and peace? Do you identify with the words listed under balance? What areas do you prefer to operate in: extreme or balance? What can you do to enhance your skills and abilities to remain in your balance?

Extremes	Balance	Extremes
Controlling	Spirit/Faith	Weak
Manipulative	Truth	Self-Sabotaging
Angry	Love	Needy
Judgmental	Knowing	Fixer
Opinionated	Wisdom	Codependent
Greed	Acceptance	Fear
Searching	Freedom	Searching
Ego	Kindness	Worry
Struggle	Creative	Struggle
Jealousy	Oneness/Balance	Envy
Pain	Peace	Pain
Abuser	Strength	Abused

Many of us operate in the extremes, and we search for things and people outside of ourselves to make us feel better about ourselves. The only real joy, peace, love, balance, and happiness you will find is not to be found on the physical realm (outside ourselves), but within you now in the spiritual realm (your faith, your balance, your core). Once you find peace, love, joy, and happiness within, it will be provided for you on the physical realm. You must become what you want. Your extremes are operated by your mind (ego, thoughts, and wants). The extremes can be deceiving, and no real good can come from them, only further pain, worry, and distrust.

When you operate within your spirit (your core, your inner knowing, your truth) and recognize and operate within your balance, the extremes have to subside, and your life will improve. We are like the pendulum on a grandfather clock swinging from one side to the other, but to get there, we must pass through our middle, our balance. If we stop swinging in the extremes and remain in the middle (the balance), this is where we will find stillness, quiet, peace, truth, love, strength, and light. It is here, within your spirit, your core, your center, that the outside extremes cannot enter, operate, or control your thinking.

SELF-REFLECTION

(This space is provided for you to reflect on
how you can apply what you've read.)

CHAPTER 9

Relationships

MY LAST RELATIONSHIP LASTED TWELVE years. I had always wanted a son but felt it would not be possible due to my lifestyle and all the chaos that had been in my life. However, when this relationship arrived in my life, it also provided me with a two-year-old son. My partner was very kind, loving, and willing to share her journey and that of her son's. This relationship settled me down in so many ways. It was a godsend in my life, showing up at the right time and for the right reasons. I had been running from myself and had no real sense of stability in my life. I had been recovering from a head injury, and I believe the relationship was placed here to provide me with stability, with love, and with the opportunity to raise a child that I had always wanted. We became a family.

Due to my history of being judged and the pain that had ensued from my past, I was never comfortable discussing my family in any circles outside of those we were close to and with people who knew us. Those inside circles were supportive of us and enjoyed the humorous and success stories we told about our son. However, it was painful to listen to people outside those intimate circles discuss their families and their children and not be able to share my own family stories with them. I would remain silent and in fear of what others would think if I openly discussed my family. People love to talk about their families and their children, and it was painful that I felt I could not do the same.

After twelve years, the relationship had become stagnant, and my partner decided to leave. Just like that, it was over. She walked out the door, took our son, and that was the end of the family I had come to love and build my life around. I had focused and given everything I could to this relationship and to our family, but somewhere I had gotten lost along the way and in process of it all. I had lost myself and had nothing left to give. I had put them first, given everything I had, built my life around them, but in the end, it was gone. The relationship was lost, and so was I.

The toll and devastation from this loss was unbearable. I felt as though a tornado had come through me and ripped my life apart, leaving it in shambles. Everything I had, everything I had worked for, and everything I believed in was gone in an instant. Just as a tornado rips a house apart, I felt as though my insides were ripped apart with nothing left standing. I didn't know where to turn, where to go, or what to do. My confidence, trust, and faith were gone. Each day seemed to drag on, and sometimes I didn't know if I would get through it. It was a struggle to be around people because the pain and loneliness were unbearable. I felt lonely when I was with others and when I was at home. There seemed to be no escape from the emptiness and pain I felt. It was a struggle to go to work or to just get through the day. I hated coming home because the house we had built was empty. I was empty. There was no one welcoming me home or asking about my day. There was no one to talk to, and no more kids coming over on the weekends. My physical house was empty, and so was my heart.

I share this with you because of the lessons I learned from this experience. I did not know it then, but it is impossible to have a healthy relationship with others (external, physical relationships) if you have not taken the time to go within and awaken to your spiritual truth. Over the years, my anger, frustration, and constant struggle in seeking something outside myself took a toll on me and on those around me. I could spend time with friends, but deep down, I was not happy and always felt there had to be something more to this thing we call life.

There had to be something more than going to work, seeking or maintaining a relationship, and paying bills. As the old saying goes: you're born, you pay taxes, and then you die. If that's truly the case, then what's the point or the purpose?

You may recall from my résumé that I spent a lot of time running from my truth and who I was. Even though I experienced rejection by others, I had begun to have my own feelings of self-rejection that I had not dealt with. I had suffered pain, judgment, humiliation, and loss, and I ran in fear in search of someone or something to fill that void. My trust in people and even in myself had been destroyed, and I feared most everyone. I carried that anger, fear, pain, and rejection for many years. My anger and fear drove me down numerous roads that usually ended in further pain, feelings of failure, and self-destruction. I had allowed others to instill fear in me years ago, and I began to think that way about myself. I hid behind a façade of acting as though I had my life together, all the while, I had this deep knowing that nothing could be further from the truth. I was not happy with myself and did not know what to do with my life. Yes, I had some good jobs and excelled in them, but I always wanted and knew there had to be more. I was always running and trying to overcompensate, hoping that others would accept me. I had the thinking that if I somehow could do more, could be more successful, could be more helpful, and could be kinder, then others would accept me.

I also mentioned in my résumé that a day came when I finally surrendered and allowed help—in the form of my trainer—to come into my life. She helped me rebuild my self-confidence, and I finally began to open up to trusting in someone again. With my trainer, there was no judgment, just understanding and a willingness to listen and help me begin taking better care of myself. She came into my life and believed in me when I did not. About this time, I had begun reading spiritual books and trying to gain some type of understanding in myself, to establish faith and to find a sense of direction. Over time, both my trainer and my readings helped me tremendously, as my physique, my confidence, my energy, and my attitude began to change.

However, there was still something more that needed to change. There was still a deep internal struggle that something was still not quite right. I still had that dark corner in my basement that I just couldn't shine a light on. That deep-seated struggle kept growing stronger and stronger and remained as pain within me. A day came when the pain seemed stronger than ever. I had taken a different route home and I noticed a sign at a church along the way, stating, "If God says it, it must be so." A few miles later, I noticed another sign, and shortly thereafter, I met my spiritual adviser. I struggled with that internal voice coaxing me to turn the car around, to surrender and to make that phone call. I am so grateful that I did because I have come to believe this was my real awakening. It was God, the internal voice, the knowing, the one who has always been here and will continue to be here, waiting for me to pay attention to the signs along my journey and to listen.

She reminded me of who I am and helped me to understand, to believe, and to stop questioning my faith, my spirit, my knowing. You see, God will always bring the right people and possibilities in your life at the right time. All you have to do is stop trying to control and fix everything and to surrender and allow for more. He provided my trainer and my spiritual adviser at the right time for the right reasons. People will show up to help us; the key is, Do we take notice, or do we push our snooze button and continue down the path of unconsciousness? My spiritual adviser and others were godsends in my life. This is what I know and I believe, and they have helped me beyond measure. At the time, I had absolutely no idea what I needed, but God did, and I was finally willing to be open and allow for it.

I have expressed key words of wisdom that you have read repeatedly throughout the previous chapters. I have stated words such as love, faith, joy, peace, positive, light, balance, wisdom, and truth. I have spoken to you using words such has God, Spirit, Source, universe, and knowing. I have discussed the difference between your internal knowing, your spirit that is comprised of love, truth, acceptance, and peace, versus the physical outside entities such as fear, anger, struggle, pain, judgment, and so on. It does not matter what word you use; it only matters that you recognize it, go within yourself to build, create, and strengthen it. The relationship category for your résumé includes your references: Who knows you? Who knows what you can do? Who believes in your skills and abilities? There are people around you right now who are willing to help you or who may need your help.

We all have varying degrees of relationships throughout our lives. However, the one true constant and primary relationship that has been here since before you were born, remains throughout your entire life, and will be there when you move on to another realm is your Source, your God, your spirit. This should be your primary relationship and be first in all your works. Your task is to learn to communicate with it, listen to it, and strengthen it. When I began to surrender, allow, and believe, my world and my life began to change for the better. This is when the right people showed up at the right time. As the fear, pain, and anger began to dissolve, my faith grew, and so did my life.

Watch the Signs

I now pay closer attention to the signs along my path. These signs may come in the form of something I read, a song on the radio, a billboard or sign that may pose some type of meaning for me, or a person that offers help or wisdom. It may also come in the form of an internal knowing and a willingness to listen to what God is telling me. I always try to remain grateful throughout my day and to allow and to be open to learning, listening, paying attention, and understanding more as I continue on my journey. This is how I continue to nurture and grow my relationship with my Source. In turn, it helps me to strengthen and grow my external relationships. Your Source is the core of your physical house (your body), and to build a house, you must first establish a strong foundation before you can build upon it. You do not need money or a college degree to begin this communication. It only takes a willingness to let go of the outside physical world and take the time to get to know and accept the truth of who you are and what you are here to do in this life. As with any relationship, you must nurture, communicate, and strengthen for it to grow and prosper.

A Time for You

You must learn to communicate and love yourself before you can truly communicate and love others. Make time for you, make time for your Source, and allow yourself to become a vessel of true, unconditional love and peace. Once you begin to faithfully practice this, you will begin to find yourself in a more peaceful, accepting, and joyful place, and in turn the outside physical things will not be so detrimental. As you awaken and become more enlightened, you will find yourself becoming a beacon of light, love, strength, and power. You will find that others will notice you and be kinder toward you as you shine and express your own light of love.

True beauty and wisdom comes from within. Your external or physical relationships will also begin to grow and become stronger as well.

Your relationship with your Source of Being is yours and yours alone. No one can take your Source from you or use it against you, for it is you and the truth of who you are. Your Source will not abandon you, reject you, leave you, or cause you pain. Your Source is based on love, truth, and wisdom. Physical entities and people may or may not remain throughout your journey, but your Source is always with you. It has always been within you, waiting patiently for you to recognize it and begin communicating and nurturing it to allow it to grow. It is the *essence* of who you truly are. No judgment or pain is in your Source, just love and peace. It has always been your choice (free will) to make the effort to communicate and nurture it or to continue to push your snooze button, ignore it, or attempt to control and search outside yourself.

Adam and Eve

One of the first known relationships was the story of Adam and Eve. God blessed them with the Garden of Eden for beauty, love, and food. They had everything they needed. The only thing God asked of them was not to eat from the tree of knowledge of good and evil. However, God gave them the choice or free will to make that decision. As long as they listened to God (their Source, their internal knowing), life was blissful, peaceful, positive, and good! God provided them with everything they needed as long as they listened and allowed. However, as we all know, the serpent (outside, physical entity) tempted Eve to eat the apple. We all know the rest of the story, but here is the point: you can go within, nurture and grow your love, truth, peace, and strength, or you can continue to seek and listen to outside forces and find shame, fear, anger, judgment, and negativity. You have been given free will—it will always be your choice.

Square Pegs and Round Holes

So how can you make a good choice? It is simple. You just need to find a peaceful, quiet place and begin to communicate by asking, listening, and continuing to nurture yourself and build your spiritual muscle. This is a growing process, a strengthening process, and a process of coming to an awareness of your truth. Any reason other than not being willing to take the time and to make the effort to meet, nurture, and grow your relationship with your Source is an excuse. Eventually we reach a point in life that we stop pushing the snooze button and awaken to the fact there must be more. It may come in the form of a painful event or loss. We may have even encountered a series of painful events and losses.

You may feel as I did and have that constant nagging pain inside that is trying to tell you something. Sometimes we finally reach the point that we no longer push our snooze button and begin to awaken and ask questions about our life. It is then that you know it is time to surrender and turn it over to your Source. It is then that you know it is time to stop holding on to anger, or controlling, or struggling and trying to fix things in your life. That job belongs to your Source! We all struggle to try to fix things ourselves or to make something work or spend our energy hoping someone will change or be a certain way. However, as the old saying goes, "You can't fit a square peg in a round hole!" Lord knows I've been guilty of trying to fix, control, or make things be a certain way throughout my life. If we used a physical example of actually trying to make a wooden square peg fit in a round hole, we would have to expend a lot of time, effort, and energy to chisel the peg to try to make it fit. You would chisel the corners and edges until it might actually go into the round hole. However, after expending all that effort and energy, what have you actually accomplished? You have tried to change the *essence* of the square peg, as it is no longer square. Now that you are finally able to make it fit, it will not stand straight but will lean or fall over. So, with all the energy and struggle you've put into this project by trying to make it fit, to control it or make it a certain way, you have changed the *essence* of what it truly is, and that is a square peg.

Do we do this in our relationships? Do we try to change the essence of others? Do we try to hide behind façades and change the essence of who we truly are? Are we allowing others to change our essence? We expend so much energy to fix or control others, and in the end, it still does not fit correctly or falls apart. I brought up this analogy to help you recognize that we do this in our lives by trying to be someone we are not. We also do this in our relationships by trying to fix others or to get others to change or to be or act a certain way. Trying to control situations or others will never work! You cannot change the essence of who you are, and you cannot change the essence of someone else. You can chisel it away, but in the end, what have you accomplished? You can allow others to chisel away at you, but in the end, what has been accomplished? You are a unique expression of God, and if you are trying to chisel your truth and hiding behind a façade, then you are diminishing yourself and God. The only way for true growth is to allow both parties in the relationship the ability to grow, share, nurture, and empower each other during your journey together. Relationships are not about trying to fix or change each other's essence. If this is the case, then eventually it will only result in bitterness and failure. Sadly, that is what happened to my relationship!

Nurturing Our Relationships

Not only do we have to recognize that our primary relationship is with our Source and we need to nurture and grow, but we also encounter various other relationships throughout our journeys. These relationships are of varying degrees and different kinds. We have relationships with our parents, siblings, and our children. We have childhood friends, first loves, pets, friends, family, best friends, partners, lovers, spouses, colleagues, clients, and more. Each relationship has its own unique purpose, and each relationship has been established between you and the other person. Just as you have your own unique relationship with your Source, you also have a unique relationship with others.

People enter our lives with different backgrounds and histories—résumés—whether it be ethnicity, race, financial status, religious beliefs, or sexual orientation. How you and that person choose to nurture and grow the relationship is a private matter. Our relationships enter our lives for love, family, friendship, employ/colleague relationships, and for lessons and growth. Our paths or our journeys have come together at the right time for the right reason. We are here to love, to learn, to teach, to share, and to help one another. We are not here to judge and discount another because of who they are or how they live their life. We have been given the choice to open up, accept, and allow ourselves to learn, to help and to support others. As long as the relationship is allowed to grow in a positive direction for both individuals, then it is based on truth, love, and acceptance for one another. On the other hand, we can remain closed in anger, fear, and judgment toward others, which will only breed more anger, intolerance, and hatred.

As I stated at the beginning of this book, we are all connected, and the way we are connected is through our Source. We are part of a whole, separated only by our physical bodies in an effort for us to create, to grow, to experience, and to learn to become more of who we truly are, and that is a beautiful, loving, physical manifestation of God. We are spiritual beings having a physical experience. How we choose to create our story (résumé), our life, our purpose, our relationships, and our experiences is up to us.

We all experience varying degrees of love, intimacy, and friendship. We also experience varying degrees of loss, pain, and sadness. These gifts of love and friendships are not placed here to try to hold, grasp, or control; rather they are provided for us to love, to share our journeys, to learn, to allow, to give, and to receive. We cannot control others. We cannot control what others choose to do or where their journey leads them. We cannot control situations or outcomes and make things be a certain way—no more than we can control day turning to night and storms, sunshine, and seasons! Remember that everything is based on energy, and energy is always flowing and moving. We can only be grateful for the time and the experience of these relationships while we share our journeys, be it days, years, or a lifetime. Begin to recognize these relationships as gifts in an effort to help you to teach, share, or learn from others.

Something Has to Change, but What?

All the love and acceptance I thought I had obtained was based on other people. If people leave your life and your shared journey ends, then what do you have? In my case, the answer was total emptiness, loss, and a feeling of failure. What did I do wrong? Could I have given more? What was wrong with me? How could this happen? This is where I began to read, to walk, and to try to find some type of meaning in my life. I didn't have the energy or the desire to spend time with or to seek others. I didn't know who I was anymore, and I sure didn't know where I fit in. This is when I really began to try to find faith and to make an effort to rebuild myself.

Deep down, I knew something had to change; in fact, I had to change. I began to take stock of my life and knew that I had run from myself for many years. I didn't have the energy or the desire to run anymore. God sat me down, and I was humbled. I had nowhere else to go, as there was no comfort in seeking people or things outside of me anymore. I had to begin to learn to take care of me. I had to find a way to begin the process of cleaning up the rubble from my tornado and then begin to seal the cracks in my foundation. Somehow, I knew if I could do that, then I could build a life that was no longer based in fear, anger, and external influences. After all these years, the memory of my grandfather's teachings about spirituality and the Bible and his phrase *faith believin'* began to resurface and resonate in my thoughts. I began to turn to God, my Source, and began a journey to make God (Spirit) my *primary* relationship. On the outside, I felt alone and abandoned, but on the inside, somehow, I still knew I wasn't alone.

After My Tornado

Over time and committed effort on both our parts, we are now friends. The partner relationship had ended, and I realize now that it was time for it to end. The energy had to be allowed to flow, to change, and to take on a different form. It took effort on both our parts to be willing to change, to reestablish, and to grow. We are now friends and have continued to coparent our son. He has remained in both of our lives and has grown into a fine young man of whom we are extremely proud.

Looking back on this experience, I recognize it as a gift that I needed to cherish, one that came into my life at the right time for the right reasons. As time goes on, I've truly learned that things change and people change, but we all must continue to move forward on our journeys. I am grateful for the relationship and all that it provided at the time and all that it continues to provide today. I had to be open and allow that relationship to take on another aspect, shape, meaning, or form. It was time. The energy had changed, and we both needed to grow. We had to move on in our journeys. When one door closes, another must open.

I am grateful that I have come through it with a greater sense of awareness, a greater knowing and a greater understanding of myself. I no longer have pain or fear but instead have been given another gift in my journey, and that has been to find me, to stop running from myself, to strengthen myself, and to help others. I have realigned my relationships and made my relationship with Source my primary relationship. I am finally finding my purpose. I have obtained a sense of happiness and peace. I have started fulfilling my dreams. I no longer feel empty and lost. I had to find it within before I could truly share it on the outside. I have come to recognize that I never found true, lasting fulfillment in other people or in things. I now know it was within me all along. I had to learn to love and accept myself before I could love and accept others, much less allow for love and acceptance to be mirrored back to me.

The Questions and the Lessons

All relationships are here for a reason, and you need to ask:

- What was I to learn from it?
- How did it strengthen me to become the person I am today?
- What lessons was I to learn from these experiences?
- How did I impact others in these relationships?
- Am I carrying anger and bitterness, or have I surrendered my anger and allowed myself to move forward on my journey?
- Was I trying to change the essence or control others?
- Did I allow others to try to change my essence or control me?

No one does things to us. They are not necessarily here to inflict pain but rather to help us to learn and to grow stronger within ourselves.

Sometimes we have to feel or to endure some pain in an effort to awaken and to grow. We are here to learn and to empower ourselves so that we may continue to grow and to help others to grow. Otherwise, we can spend our lives continuously seeking outside of ourselves and continue to repeat the same old behaviors or patterns, and in turn, we will continue to receive the same or similar outcomes. Are we in a pattern of continuing to do the same thing and expecting different results? We must find our truth and love ourselves; then the right people will show up to share their truth and their love with us. If we try to hold or control others, then we are only hurting ourselves and sabotaging both parties in the relationship.

We are here to share and experience our journeys and to love one another. However, when it is time to continue our journeys, we must be willing to accept it, to allow for the energy to change, to grow, and to move forward. We cannot continue to grasp or hold on to one another. If we find ourselves in a relationship that may be unhappy, unhealthy, abusive, or toxic, then we are only continuing to hurt ourselves and the other party by remaining stagnant and in a state of struggle, fear, worry, pain, and grief. We are trying to grasp, control, or hold on to an energy force that cannot be contained. In this case, each person in the relationship needs to be willing to work to make efforts to grow and nurture their primary relationship with their Source and secondarily work on the physical relationship. If the two parties in the physical relationship are unwilling to do this, likely the physical relationship will continue to deteriorate or end. In this situation, we've expended a tremendous amount of time and energy trying to control, fix, or change someone that was never ours to change, or we have lost our true self in the process. If this type of relationship brings out the worst in each person, then what is it accomplishing? How are we growing within our selves? Are we holding on to something that we are afraid to let go of? If so, what is driving that fear? God wants us to love and be happy. If this type relationship is not providing that, then maybe it's time to review: what is the fear-based driving force behind it?

We cannot put our entire being into someone else in an effort to hold on to or to keep them with us. If we continue to do this, then we have once again taken the focus off of our primary relationship and placed our focus outside of us, on someone else. If we place all our focus on another person and that person leaves, then where will we be? Who will we be? Everyone must be allowed to grow, learn, and experience. We are all made up of energy and are not to be controlled or grasped. We are here to share our experiences, to recognize who we are, not to make others be a certain way or allow others to try to change our own essence.

Oftentimes we find ourselves seeking and searching for someone else to help complete us or make us whole. We feel alone or incomplete within our own selves and have a belief that someone else on the outside is going to be all we will need to fulfill that internal longing. What we are really feeling is the need to recognize and believe in our own true selves and build our love and acceptance from within. This is the *only* thing that will truly fill that void or that longing. Then you will have everything you need when the right person comes into your life to build a lasting, strong, loving, healthy relationship. You must become what you want and work to become whole within yourself before you have true love and compassion to give and receive.

Many people go from one relationship to another, thinking, *Maybe this will be the person to complete my life*. We're continuously searching outside ourselves to fill that need of love and acceptance. The outside physical newness will always wear off, and eventually we find ourselves seeking someone or something else to make us feel better or worthy. The whole time, you have carried it inside of you, and it never cost you a dime.

No matter how many directions or roads I went down, searching for the next person or thing to fill that void, that longing, that pain, I recognize now that my Source was with me all along and never once abandoned me. You must build, strengthen, and love yourself to feed your need for love, acceptance, belonging, peace, and truth. Nothing outside of that will ever give you the lasting peace, love, and contentment you are so desperately seeking. Once you do this, begin to feel it and establish your truth and love within, everything on the outside is like the icing on the cake. It *will* be provided to you and be sweeter than ever before! I had often wondered what would it feel like to be truly happy, peaceful, accepted, and loved. Once I set out on the journey of true change within, this is when I truly began to recognize and feel those answers.

I have worked in an inpatient psychiatric facility and have worked with many children from broken homes. They were abused and desperately wanted someone to love and accept them. They wanted love and acceptance but had no idea how to obtain it. They did not feel worthy within themselves and searched for someone to fill the void from the outside. They would cry and beg for someone to love them and in the next minute would sabotage themselves and act out in extreme anger and violence. They were conditioned to think that having sex would provide them with love and acceptance. However, what they received was a continuous cycle of abuse, rejection, anger, and fear. They also thought that if they were able to get pregnant and have a child, that the child would heal their pain and that they would receive the love and acceptance they so desperately longed for from that child.

They had no self-confidence and no real feeling of hope and love. Their lives were based in fear, anger, pain, and desperation—always seeking someone or something to make them feel better. This may be an extreme situation as an example of seeking people and things outside of us to make us feel loved and accepted and to have a sense of belonging. However, I used this example because I want you to realize that love and acceptance cannot be found by seeking outside ourselves. We must find our strength and love within, and then it will be provided for us on the outside.

Over the years, I've observed couples who were having difficulty in their marriages or relationships. They didn't want to let their relationships fall apart but did not have the strength, peace, and love to work on them, nurture them, or maintain them. They tried to control or fix the relationship, all the while not focusing or involving their Source. Their answer would be to consider having a baby in an effort to make their relationship work. Were these couples searching for something or someone outside themselves in hopes to somehow magically make their marriages or their relationships work?

Once you build your strength and light, the right people will be attracted to you. These are the people who don't want to change, control, or make you someone you are not. You will have your own strength and love. You will have feelings of confidence and empowerment within that will cause you to no longer feel the need to change or control others. These are the people who will accept you and help you to become an even better person. In turn, you will help them. These will be healthy, nurturing, strong relationships.

Maybe you've heard or recognize these statements: surround yourself with successful people, and you will be successful; surround yourself with positive people, and you will be more positive, fulfilled, and joyful. If you build upon your own strengths and keep faith, then the right people will be attracted to you, and all you have to do is show up. Then, there will be no more struggling in negativity, fear, and distrust. The people that do not benefit you or are toxic in your life will go their own way, or you will remove yourself from them. Someday, those unhealthy people may see your strength, your growth and positive changes, which in turn may be the lightbulb to help them awaken. However, it is not your responsibility to try to do it that for them. In fact, you can't; it's impossible. People awaken in their own time, when they are ready and when they get tired of pushing their snooze button. If you are awakening and beginning to grow and yet still trying to fix or control another person in an effort for them to grow, then you are only hindering yourself and your well-being. You must maintain and strengthen your primary relationship and, in turn, allow others to discover theirs.

Everybody has something to offer. Everybody has their own unique expression of life. Anyone you encounter throughout your day could be the one person that needs your smile and kind words, or maybe you recognize and show gratitude when others provide it to you. Everyone is here to teach us something or to learn something from us. The lesson may come in the form of a business relationship, an intimate relationship, a friend relationship, or even that brief stranger that you pass in a parking lot or the person waiting on you behind the checkout counter.

Positivity is contagious, just like negativity. It is your choosing as to which wolf you feed and how you choose to live, create, and build your life. It is your choosing to remain in unhealthy relationships or to let go, to find your strength, to grow, and to move forward. You always have the power of now to take this opportunity to light the spark inside of you and grow!

Modeling Positive Relationships for Our Children

As stated earlier, we cannot control anyone or anything, and this is true in every relationship that we have. This is also true for our children. We are here to teach and model positive behaviors. If we only try to oversee and control our children, we will instill fear, stagnation, and unhealthy or acting-out behaviors. Our children also have their Source of Being—their internal knowing. One of the best things we can do is nurture our Source within ourselves so we can model it for our children. This is how we help them to believe, to grow and to have a positive, healthy, creative, and productive life. We need to allow them to expand upon their own creativity, to find their own passion and their own unique expression of self.

As I have changed, I have begun to model these behaviors for our son. I believe he recognizes the changes that I have made and that it has strengthened our relationship. Although, like any parent, we don't always agree with the choices our kids make, I've come to recognize that we cannot be with them 24-7 to make their choices for them. What we can do is model, teach, love, and respect them. We cannot hold on to, control, or force them to be a certain way. As with energy, when you apply force, you will receive counterforce. Help them find, strengthen, and maintain their internal sense of knowing. Help them to recognize and make better choices when negative influences and forces come along during their journey.

You are here to teach, to support, and to help them work through their growing and learning processes. They need to be allowed to find their unique expression and build upon it. Teach them, model positivity for them, help them, support them, but most of all, love and accept them for who they are. They were not placed here for us to try to control, or to make them be a certain way, or to accomplish certain things that we *think* they should accomplish. If this is what we do to our children, then we are back to trying to control others. We should help them to understand better choices, but we must model it as well. Help them to find and establish their creativity and provide for them encouragement, love, and acceptance for all they are and for all they may accomplish. Do not chisel away their essence but allow them to find their passion and their creativity. Allow them to grow. If we have established our truth, our love, our essence, and have become accepting of who we are, then we can easily model that for our children, our partner, and our other relationships.

Uniquely You

You need to love and accept yourself because you are a unique expression of God. If you do this, you will make better, more confident, wiser choices. You will be more loving, accepting, and nurturing in your relationships. Again, it all begins from within, and by taking the steps to develop and improve your relationship with your Source of Being, your life, your relationships, and how you act and respond to experiences will begin to change and improve.

I wanted to share the following poem with you, as I refer to it often throughout my day. You can read it and apply it to yourself or you can read it and apply it to those with whom you have a relationship. It is about letting go and not trying to control outcomes.

It is a poem by Naomi Long Madgett:

Woman with Flower

I wouldn't coax the plant if I were you. Such watchful nurturing
may do it harm. Let the soil rest from so much digging
The leaf's inclined to find its own direction; Give it a chance
to seek the sunlight for itself. Much growth is stunted
by too careful prodding, Too eager tenderness.
The things we love we have to learn to leave alone.

SELF-REFLECTION

(This space is provided for you to reflect on
how you can apply what you've read.)

CHAPTER 10

Mirrors

"NO MATTER WHERE YOU GO ... there you are." Our lives are like mirrors. Who you are on the inside and what you exhibit to the outside world is a direct reflection of what you see and receive. True beauty and love and acceptance come from within. In the physical world, you can stand in front of a mirror and see with your physical eyes a direct reflection of your physical self. This is also true for the spiritual mirror. Your spiritual mirror is a direct reflection of how you think, feel, and act in the spirit, and it reflects what you receive and experience.

In comparison to your physical résumé, this may fall under the category of your work history. What work have you done in the past and how has that reflected back to you? What work are you doing today in regards to your life? If we stand in front of a physical mirror and look at ourselves, we are often very critical of what we see. Some of us refuse to even look in the mirror for that very reason! For example, we critique our hair, our looks, our wrinkles, our weight, and everything based on our physical appearance. How often do you stand in front of the physical mirror and identify, accept, and admire your positive qualities? Do you ever look past your physical aspects and go within to find your spiritual mirror to see and admire the true beauty of who you truly are?

Remember—what you think about expands and will come back to you multiplied. For example, if you choose to think and live in lack, then you will receive more of the same, and that is lack. If you are critical of yourself, then you will give and receive criticism. If you always feel there is never enough or wonder when will you win the lottery, or feel you have to constantly struggle, then you will continue to remain in that pattern. As long as you think this way, it will be mirrored back to you as struggle, lack, and never enough.

That leads to a telling question: exactly what is enough? If you are not clear about being grateful and thinking and believing that you already have what you need, then you will always be striving for more. If you remain in the cycle of always striving for more, then when will it ever be enough? Your focus remains on having more or never having enough, and you are not being grateful for what you currently have. If you cannot be grateful for what you have, such as your health, your beauty, your love, and the gifts in your life, then you will always think you need more, and you will always receive never enough. You are back to the cycle of striving and never arriving. It is truly being reflected back to you. By doing this, you are diminishing your self- worth, your health, your confidence, and your strength. You are wasting your energy and turning your power over to outside forces beyond your control.

When we are worried about others' opinions of us, we allow fear-based thinking to sabotage us. We must let go of negative, fear-based, angry, opinionated, judgmental thinking that no longer serves us and stop living in our mind (ego) thoughts. Some of us sabotage ourselves by always looking for sympathy and feeling our world is ending. We have the "woe is me" attitude. Some of us think and say such things as, "Anything that can go wrong in my life will go wrong." Or, "With my luck, it will never happen." Some of us remain in a victim role just to get sympathy or attention. What does this type of thinking provide for you? Is this really the type of negative attention you want? Has this been the basis of your work history?

Attention and acceptance are two different things, so you must be clear on what you want. Are you looking for attention, or do you really want to feel accepted and loved? You must focus on you, your spirit and your thoughts and actions. Sometimes we feed off others' sympathy in hopes of finding acceptance, but what we are actually receiving is attention. If you are looking for attention and sympathy, then you are relying on physical, outside people and influences to provide that for you. This will never last, as people go back to their respective lives and you are still alone, wallowing in self-pity, searching for more attention.

Is your work history based on obtaining attention? Does attention give you what you need? Could you be confusing attention for acceptance? We see our young people dressing all in black, coloring or spraying their hair. We see piercings and tattoos. We see them using more drugs in an effort to fit in, or thinking that the outside physical things and appearance will get them noticed or make them stand out from the crowd. They too arrived with a knowing, but somehow we instilled the outside, physical things upon them and taught them these behaviors. Would it be safe to say they are really looking for love and acceptance and somehow confused it for attention based on physical looks and appearance? Could it be that they are not finding, strengthening, and applying their own unique skills and abilities?

I have said repeatedly that you must recognize your Source and obtain true love and acceptance for yourself; then you will have obtained lasting strength, love, confidence, and truth. Once you have established love and acceptance for who you are, you will have love and acceptance to share with others. In turn, others will mirror love and acceptance back to you. You no longer need to seek attention, for you will give and receive acceptance. Some of us feel that when things are going well in our life, it will only be a matter of time before the other shoe will drop. We spend our energy wondering how long it will last or even feel that we don't deserve this wonderful gift. If we have this type of thinking, then eventually, it will be lost or deflected from us.

We thought and felt we didn't deserve it, and so it was! Your spiritual mirror deflected it from you. What purpose is this thinking providing you? What are you gaining from it? Better yet—what have you lost from it? Can you identify an event in your life when this has happened? We have all done this, and likely, we can now identify the pain, struggle, or short-lived attention that came from the loss. We don't seem to learn from what is truly happening with our thoughts and actions. We all want to feel love and acceptance. Yet, to feel the true love and acceptance by others, we must first begin to feel love and acceptance within our own selves. We must look at our spiritual mirror, build our spiritual muscle, and focus on what we need and be grateful for who we are and what we have. We have to be careful that we don't miss the point of building our spiritual muscle.

We need to love and accept ourselves for the truth of who we are and why we are here. Once we establish and build upon our own feelings of love, acceptance, confidence, strength, and worthiness, we will become stronger, kinder, more loving, and more peaceful. We no longer want or need to seek attention. We will become less concerned about others' opinions. Our positive thoughts and actions will begin to improve. To use a cliché, the glass will become half-full instead of half-empty. If you are not willing to grow, appreciate, nurture, and be grateful for the things you currently have right now in your life, those things will be removed or deflected from you.

If you go inside and begin to seek and work with your Source of Being, you will change the way you view yourself from the inside (spiritual mirror), and it will start to reflect on the outside. You will find that people treat you differently because you are treating yourself differently. Your internal light will become brighter, and others will begin to take notice. They may ask if you have done something different to your hair or remark that somehow you look different. They will begin to take notice of you and treat you with kindness. You may even begin to notice strangers smiling at you and being kind. You will be carrying yourself with a confidence and a light that will become your own true secret. You will smile at others, be grateful for their kindness, and know in your heart that the true change is coming from within—that your light is getting stronger. Once you begin to find love, beauty, peace, respect, knowing, joy, and abundance within yourself, then the lack, problems, worry, opinions, judgment, and struggle will gradually cease.

You have all you need within you right now to grow. The rest will reflect upon itself with your spiritual mirror and be provided for you. This is what will be mirrored back to you. If you are angry, struggling, negative, and judgmental, always wanting what someone else has, then you are not in tune with your Source of Being. You will continue to remain in a state of negativity, unfulfillment, and struggle until you change yourself from the inside out. No one can provide it for you, no one can do it for you, and no one owes it to you! This is your journey, and only you can establish, nurture, and strengthen your relationship with yourself and your Source. The best news is that it does not cost a dime and is available to you at a moment's notice no matter what time of the day or night. The only thing you have to do is surrender, allow, and make the effort to do it.

Take the opportunity to look at yourself in the spiritual mirror and say positive things about yourself. Look beyond your physical self. Let go of criticizing yourself. Become kind and loving, for you are a unique being and physical manifestation of God. You are special, and you are here for a purpose; we *all* are. Begin your affirmations. Even if you don't truly believe these statements at first, say them until you do. Be loving, kind, and respectful to yourself, and in turn, you are being loving, kind, and respectful to your Source. Anything other than positive statements and affirmations about yourself are a direct reflection and diminishing of yourself, which is your Source—God! There are many ways to do this. When I was at my lowest point and felt I had nothing left, this is what I did:

- I began walking and saying affirmations to myself. It was hard for me to believe the affirmations at first, but I kept faith and practicing until I began to feel it and believe it.
- I would go for a walk and state in my mind, that *I am* beautiful, *I am* strong, *I am* loving, *I am* kind, *I am* abundant, *I am* successful, *I am* prosperous, *I am* grateful.
- I would come up with these statements, and I began to find other positive words to use throughout my walk.
- I would look at the sky, the sun, nature, and everything around me. I became more observant of nature, of God.
- I started to find gratitude for being alive and began to recognize that God is in everything. Being outside and observing nature and smiling or speaking to others who were on their walks gave me strength and hope.
- I would repeat affirmations in my mind throughout my entire walk.
- I would repeat the affirmations during my drive to work until it became a big part of my day and thought process.

As I remained faithful, I began to see and feel a change in my energy. I began to let go of the fear and critical thinking. I found myself becoming stronger. I became more consciously aware of how I treated myself and how I treated others around me. Affirmations became the key toward true transformation in my life. I learned that affirmations are not based on what others think of me. Affirmations were the keys to helping me believe in myself. Affirmations nourished my spirit and helped me build my spiritual muscle.

When you begin a daily regime of affirmations, you too will begin to believe and feel them and open yourself up to true change and transformation in your life. Your thinking will improve, and you will grow stronger. Now you are looking into your spiritual mirror with love and acceptance. Your thinking, your faith, and your believing will begin to change, and so will the events reflected back to you. Once you begin to see these differences, you will come to realize your spirit is getting stronger, and your thoughts and actions are improving. You are improving, gaining strength, and growing. This is true empowerment. This is true enlightenment. This improves your world and the world reflected back to you.

As you awaken and become more observant of your thoughts and actions, you will also realize your mind and physical body will have no other option but to change as well. You will realize that you are taking better care of your physical self because it is your home for your Source while you are here on this physical journey. You may find yourself more willing to take care of your body, to exercise and to have better nutrition. You will see that "positive in" will reflect as "positive out." Begin with your spirit, and you will find your mind (thoughts, ego) begin to change, and your body (physical home) will begin to change as well. Nurturing and strengthening your spirit will nurture and strengthen your mind, and in turn, your body will follow. The world around you will begin to change and improve because you have made a choice and an effort to change and improve. The negativity and stressors of the day will not have such a profound effect on you. You will see and act differently with strength, love, and confidence. You will become more aware and observant of the miracles and wonderful gifts provided to you. You will also be more conscious to accept your gifts with love, peace, and gratitude. You will be more consciously aware and observant of the beauty within you and the beauty that surrounds you. You will be more loving, creative, accepting, and tolerant with less negativity, control, and struggle.

You will become your own creative, abundant, beautiful source of light, love, and peace. All it takes is you having faith and surrendering to loving and accepting your own self, your own Source of Being. Your spiritual mirror will reflect positive, good, and great things back to you, for that is who you are and who you are becoming. No money, no amount of struggle, no anger, no control, just a newfound way of living and finding peace, love, joy, acceptance, and happiness. You will have more quality time and will appreciate your relationships, and you will have the willingness and the energy to nurture and grow them.

You no longer need to sweat the small stuff of daily life in the physical world, such as external problems or events beyond your control. You no longer will seek attention, for you have recognized the difference and obtained your own acceptance and empowerment. The negative things will lose their power over you, because your spiritual mirror will deflect them. In turn, you will become more creative, happy, productive, grateful, and more aware of what is truly important in your life. This is your purpose—to find, love, accept, develop, create, and cocreate with your Source of Being and to become a wonderful, unique expression of God. You are a unique vessel of light and love. Once you do this, practice it, build your strength, and keep your faith, then the possibilities are unlimited. This is true power. This is true strength. Your thinking and priorities will change, and you will come to meet and to know your true self.

Let me be clear: this is not about winning millions in the weekly lottery. This is about looking in the mirror, coming to the truth of who you are, opening up, and allowing for great things to flow in and through your life. It's about faith, truth, building strength, accepting and loving yourself. It's about sharing it with others, and in turn, all this will be reflected back to you. When you build your spiritual muscle and begin giving and receiving love, truth, acceptance, and gratitude, then you have won your own lottery!

SELF-REFLECTION

(This space is provided for you to reflect on
how you can apply what you've read.)

CHAPTER 11

Acts of Kindness

IT IS TIME TO FIND your truth and obtain a beautiful, abundant life of your own. Everything you've done in your life, every person you have met, loved, worked with, every experience you have gone through has led you to here and now. It is time to review your life and bring it into clearer focus so you may move forward in a better and stronger capacity. For your résumé, this chapter would be based on your work experience. What work have you done in the past and what are you doing now?

This chapter is titled "Acts of Kindness" because it is imperative that you recognize and perform acts of kindness during your day. As with everything else I've discussed, there is no financial obligation for performing acts of kindness. Some of the things I am about to mention, you may already do throughout your day, but are you consciously aware and do you recognize that you are doing them? Maybe you think you're being kind, but are you consciously aware of your actions and what you do throughout your day? How are you helping? How are you impacting others? Many of us get so caught up in our own daily routines and our own self-centeredness that we don't think about or recognize the effect we may have on others. This chapter is to awaken you, bringing about a conscious awareness of what you are doing, how you are acting, and how you may be perceived by others.

The time you spend in the morning getting ready for work, getting the kids off to school, driving in traffic—whatever the case may be—can be a make or break point of your day. Sometimes you wake up late, have a sick child, try to find daycare, get stuck in traffic, and are late to work. What is your energy and what kind of tone have you set for yourself and those around you on that day? Things happen, and that's part of life. How you choose to handle these challenging situations is completely up to you. You can get upset and honk your horn at everyone on the road and cut in and out of traffic. You can exhibit anger to your child (who is already not feeling well and feeling your frustration). You can be rude to your colleagues when you finally arrive at work. Those choices already set the tone for the day that everyone needs to steer clear of you because you're in a terrible mood. You've not only destroyed these moments in your day, increased your blood pressure, anxiety level, and anger, but you've infringed upon and possibly lashed out on those around you. How have you impacted others?

Identify your own energy for that situation and how that impacted you. You've lost your balance and centeredness, and you separated yourself from your Source of Being. You did this all by your choice, your free will. No one did anything to you. No one made your child sick. No one made you late for work. You chose to be angry, to lash out and to infringe upon others, including the strangers on the road that you chose to honk your horn at and cut off in traffic. This is a lesson in becoming consciously aware of your energy and what you are doing at any given moment, on any given day, and recognizing the choices you are making and the effect or impact these choices have upon you and those around you.

Let's take the same scenario and change the energy and the choice. You take some deep breaths, call to let your supervisor or coworker know what is going on and that you will be there as soon as you can. You comfort your child who is not feeling well. You've now taken responsibility for the events that are taking place. You're not getting angry or anxious, increasing your blood pressure or taking your frustrations out on anyone who comes into your vicinity. You attempt to do one thing at a time, and you work to keep your balance while achieving the goals of obtaining childcare, showing love to your child— not frustration, and you still make it to work.

In both scenarios, you arrived at work, but this way you arrived at work safely without negatively impacting everyone in your way, so why not do it in a manner that is kinder, more balanced, and healthier? Once you arrive at work, you can discuss your hectic morning and maybe even laugh at the craziness of it all. You can state that you made it and you're prepared to move on with your day in a more positive and productive manner.

This scenario is just one example of a life event that will happen in one form or another. Your test of strength comes from how you handle the challenges. By your choice, the outcome can be one of inflicting havoc on yourself and others, with possible regrets for your actions, or it can be one of kindness, empathy, peace, and understanding. You make the choice, and you receive the reward or the consequence. What you do on the inside is what is mirrored back to you on the outside.

Too often, we get so wrapped up in our hurried, rushed, and busy lives that we forget to provide a simple act of kindness to someone. As I've continued to grow on my journey, I make a point every day to ensure I provide a heartfelt act of kindness and show gratitude to others who come along my path. I've begun to take notice of someone waiting on me at the checkout counter or the drive-through and make an effort to catch their eyes and show them a heartfelt thank you and appreciation. It's amazing how I've begun to see their expression change when I do this. All it took was a small moment of time to show someone I was paying attention and that I took interest in them. I provided gratitude for what they were doing to help me. When I see their expression change and a heartfelt smile come from them, it has just been mirrored back to me, and both our hearts were lifted in that brief moment.

I make it part of my daily mission to be kind and appreciative to everyone I see, and I so enjoy the positive change in their expression. I always walk away with a smile in my heart and a smile on my face, knowing I shined my light of love and they saw it.

You may have noticed that I used the word *namaste* in the introduction. I love this word, I believe in this word, and I love using and performing it. It has various meanings, such as a greeting or salutation. It is also "a representation of the divine in me recognizes the divine in you in a place where we are all one." By performing these acts of kindness, I feel and witness namaste daily. This becomes an act of validating the other person. They realize they have been seen, noticed, and recognized and feel in that moment that they matter. How many of us want or need validation? If fact, could you say that validation is providing a form of acceptance? I think so.

I also want you to be consciously aware of your acts of kindness and gratitude each day. If you are not finding ways to exhibit acts of kindness and gratitude, then you are truly missing out on substantial growth, strength, and love in your life. Acts of kindness are not conditional and don't necessarily cost money. We don't provide acts of kindness with the thinking, *If I do this for this person, then maybe they will do something for me.* You cannot place conditions on acts of kindness. They are given from your heart because you feel the need to or just want to.

Acts of kindness can come in many forms and can be given to anyone at any time. You can provide acts of kindness to strangers you meet on the street or in a parking lot. You can provide acts of kindness to your family, friends, and all your various relationships. Acts of kindness are a gift of your love and kindness and are a selfless act. When you give acts of kindness, you receive heart-lifting love multiplied back to you. Anything given with love and kindness without conditions can be considered an act of kindness. Here are just a few examples:

- a hug, just because
- eye contact to include a smile and a friendly hello when you pass or see a stranger
- holding a door open for someone and smiling
- giving someone something that has importance and meaning to you
- picking up the phone or making an effort to visit a
- friend or loved one
- volunteering for a worthy cause
- putting in a good word for someone
- listening to or helping someone in need

There are many ways you can incorporate acts of kindness throughout your day. The reward is how good it makes you feel. This also opens you up to receive acts of kindness from others. Pay it forward and be aware that you are consciously doing this every day until it becomes a part of who you are, what you do, and how you believe.

What will you do today to provide an act of kindness to someone? Be consciously aware that you are doing this and realize that eye contact is extremely important. Looking down, saying thanks, and continuing on with your hurried, busy life is not an act of kindness. They say the eyes are the windows to the soul. When you catch someone's eyes and give a heartfelt thank you, a "have a nice day," and a smile, this is when you observe their facial expression change as they realize someone is kind and does care. This is when you will know namaste: the divine in me recognizes the divine in you as we meet in a place where we are one. And this is when you truly know you have made a loving, kind, positive impact at that very moment.

SELF-REFLECTION

(This space is provided for you to reflect on
how you can apply what you've read.)

CHAPTER 12

Judgment

I WOULD BE REMISS IF I did not bring this chapter into this book. Judgment is something we all do and have also been the recipient of at one time or another in our lives. When we arrive as an infant on our journeys, we arrive with our internal knowing, our spirit, which is based on love, light, acceptance, and goodness, and it guides us through our growing process. In infancy, we have no idea about fear, money, greed, power, worry, stress, control, judgment, material possessions, race, sex, religion, anger, and violence. These are learned behaviors that have been taught to us and instilled in our mind (ego, thoughts, and opinions). This has all been told to us or modeled for us by others. For your résumé, this would correspond to your educational history.

When it comes to judgment, what has been your educational history?

- What were you taught by others?
- Does your educational history lean toward negative, judgmental, fear-based, intolerant influences? If so, what have you been taught?
- Who taught you this way of living and believing?
- How have these teachings impacted your life?
- Are you continuing to teach and model the same to others?
- How has your education and judgment impacted the lives of others?
- Do judgment and blame make you feel more important, more in charge, or better than others?

Perhaps your educational history leans toward more positive, open, loving, and accepting influences and behavior. If that is the case, consider your answer to these questions:

- What have you been taught?
- Who taught you this way of living and believing?
- Are you continuing to teach and model the same to others?
- How have these teachings impacted your life?
- How have these teachings impacted the lives of others?

A few years ago, I heard this: a positive person is a negative person's teacher, and a negative person is a positive person's job. Where do you find yourself in that statement? How has your life been impacted by judgment, blame, criticism, and negativity? How have you impacted others by judging, blaming, criticizing, and negativity?

Judgment comes in many forms, and we should also be aware that when we judge, we tend to first label and then categorize everyone and everything. First, we label someone, and then we place them into a certain category and try to make them fit in that category. If someone does something bad, we tend to label and then categorize that person in with others. Or we may even go so far as to categorize their family or those close to them. It's time to recognize that no one's life is perfect, not even ours. Everyone has his or her journey. It's time we stop trying to label and categorize everyone based on our thinking and opinions.

One form of judgment is the opinionated thinking and envy toward others who we think may have the "perfect life." We seem to envy those who have a good job, financial stability, a beautiful family, a big job title, fame, fancy cars, and so on. This thinking (opinion) is based on physical possessions and appearances. However, nothing is ever how it appears. We may also judge, label, and categorize those people as spoiled or manipulative. Sometimes we even make unkind remarks like, "They must have slept their way to the top!" Or, "Who did they steal from to achieve that?" We waste a tremendous amount of our energy and time wanting what others have, and in turn, we take the focus off ourselves and lose sight of our own lives. We need to come to the realization of who we are, become aware of what we have accomplished in our own lives, and be grateful for the gifts (skills and abilities) we possess. We can sit around wishing, hoping, wanting, envying, and even blaming others for what they have, how they live, or what they do, but that will always lead us down a dead-end road with no resolution and no real change for our own lives. It is time to stop judging and blaming others for who they are, what they do, how they live, how they look, or for what they've accomplished or may even possess.

I have been judged on many occasions, but the one that most affected my life was when I was judged not on my job performance but for whom I loved. Although it's been many years since I was judged, labeled, and categorized, it was devastating then, and it is still unsettling to witness how people judge others. I am not a label, nor a job title, nor a ranking or number on a spreadsheet, nor to be placed in a category based on someone's opinion, fear, and judgment over things they do not know or understand. I am so much more. We all are!

My experience was such a turning point in my life. I cannot begin to tell you the impact of pain, hurt, and fear it caused me. I was always worrying about what others might think. I was doing what I thought others thought I should do. Yet I was searching here and there to find acceptance, to be successful and do the right thing in my life and career. I've always been a kind and loving individual with a big heart and have never been one to intentionally cause fear or pain to someone or something else. I did everything in my power to do the right thing so others would not hate me, turn their back on me, or reject me. I just wanted to live my life in peace and to be accepted for the person I was. I wanted to be loved and accepted.

I mentioned earlier that we arrive with our DNA, which provides our looks and our given name, but we are all so much more, and I've come to realize this in my journey. However, I allowed others' opinions and judgments—and even endured physical violence that came from the fear and judgment of a few—to cause such an impact on my life that I spent years trying to hide, control, fix, overcompensate, and mask the pain and fear in my own life. I expended a tremendous amount of energy over the years, running, hiding, and living in fear of judgment and rejection. I could not discuss my family or my life for fear of being judged, mistreated, or rejected or losing clients or my job.

Sadly, I must admit to you that I too have judged others. I recognize this was my choice based on my own fear and pain, and it was mirrored back to me in the form of more fear, struggle, and pain. I refused to allow others to get close to me and could not be honest with them for fear that I would be rejected. The fact of the matter is I was judging and predetermining what I thought others' opinions and responses toward me would be, because of what I had endured in my past. I sabotaged myself and missed out on possible opportunities for positive, healthy relationships. My judgment was mirrored back to me, and I remained in fear of what others might think. I didn't believe in myself, so why should anyone else? Because of what I endured in the past—by the actions of a few people—I judged and believed that everyone would judge me and treat me just as harshly. I was filled with fear and distrust, and I too categorized that others would judge and treat me the same as the few I had endured from my past.

I've come to realize that we seem to listen to or follow the negative, fear-based words of a few. We then follow suit and form more negative opinions based on others' statements. Then we begin grouping all people associated with that judgment into one category. We form opinions of people and things, based on fear of what we don't know or understand. When do we as individuals recognize our own selves (love and strength), allowing for growth, love, truth, and understanding? When do we stop basing our love, truth, and acceptance on the negative thoughts and opinions of others? When do we begin to open our hearts and minds and go within to spirit and our own answers and truth?

Everything Is Not Always as It Seems

Allow me to share a recent experience with you. I was preparing to write this chapter and had been asking Spirit to give me help. I've mentioned numerous times in this book that everything happens at the right time for the right reason. On this day, I believe this experience came to me at the right time and for the right reason.

I was sitting in a physician's office waiting to be called back to see the doctor. It was a specialist's office, so the people in the waiting room were not physically ill and feeling bad. The waiting area was full, and people were sitting and conversing with one another. I was sitting on a double-seated bench observing others and thinking about this chapter when I noticed an elderly man walk in and go straight to the restroom.

It was very cold outside, and he was dressed in an old, raggedy coat and pants. He had a scraggly white beard and looked like he might be homeless and had just walked in off the street to use the restroom. I observed the looks and actions of those around me. The conversations they had been involved in had suddenly stopped as they looked over and watched him. You could see the discomfort in their looks and actions. I too wondered about him walking into this office and going directly to the restroom. He didn't appear to fit in with the rest of us.

Aside from that, I also felt empathy and concern and wondered about how the homeless actually survive in cold weather. I recognized in that very moment we all had judged and categorized him. A few minutes later, he returned from the restroom, went to the receptionist's window, and signed in. Apparently, he belonged here after all. I still noticed the others stare and then look away as to ignore him when he walked over to the waiting area in an effort to find a seat. I became intrigued as I observed the atmosphere of the room change.

As he walked over to the waiting area and looked around, he suddenly turned, walked directly over to me, and stated, "I know I look funny, but I don't bite. Do you mind if I sit here beside you?" I said, "Sure, I don't mind at all." I moved over on the bench so he could sit beside me. I observed the others start to stare again as he sat down beside me, and I could feel their discomfort. The moment he sat down, he politely introduced himself to me and said, "I used to be clean shaven and wear those three-piece monkey suits, but as you can see, I don't do that anymore. I gave up that crazy corporate stuff years ago." I began to chuckle. Now I was really intrigued! I had a feeling I was about to learn something, at the right time and for the right reason.

I asked what he used to do. I also noticed out of the corner of my eye the others' ears began to perk up and listen. I noticed the others start to glance in our direction and then quickly look away again. I could tell they were curious too. He told me he was a retired university professor, a dean for his department. He began to tell me what he had done during that time to improve life in our local community—things from twenty years ago. He had worked with law enforcement and with our state legislature to promote safer and better laws. He mentioned legislative names from years ago and stated how he had come to know them, work with them, and help develop improved options for our community. You can imagine my intrigue as I listened to his story (a brief synopsis of his résumé) and observed the others around us begin to watch and listen as well.

A few minutes later, I was called to go back to see the doctor. I was enjoying this conversation and learning from him and did not want to leave. I shook his hand, looked him in the eyes with validation (expressed my namaste), and told him what a pleasure it was to have the opportunity to meet and talk with him. He acknowledged me with the same, and I knew in that moment that we had connected to the essence of one another.

As I walked away, there was pure joy in my heart. I had been provided with the opportunity to recognize judgment and fear in action. I had been given the opportunity to actually meet and go beyond the surface of this man's current physical appearance and connect with the truth and beauty within. I had been able to see that we all have unique skills and abilities and that this man had made good use of his. I had received confirmation that we all have our own stories, our own résumé, and if we just take the opportunity to go beyond the physical, we just may learn something!

As you can see, I had judged this man as homeless when he walked in. I'm pretty sure by observing those around me that they did the same. When he walked into the waiting room, people stared and quickly looked away. I observed dis-ease, maybe some fear or a feeling of being uncomfortable in the eyes and actions of those around me. Why were they feeling that way? What had this man done to make them uncomfortable? Could it have simply been because of his physical appearance? He certainly had not threatened them. He walked into the office just the same as the rest of us. He was there for an appointment to see the doctor just as we were. For whatever reason, he came straight toward me to sit down. Maybe, somehow he felt led to come and sit with me. Maybe he saw my light and my balance. Maybe he somehow knew I didn't seem threatened by him. Maybe he felt he needed to speak to me.

I believe everything happens for a reason, and it really doesn't matter how it happened; the fact is that it happened. I believe I needed to meet him and to hear his story. I needed to understand my own sense of judgment and to observe the actions of those around me. I needed to share this experience with you in this chapter. Because of his appearance, I knew he had been grouped into a category by most everyone in the room. Could he be homeless? Could he be dangerous? Could they "catch" something from him? What about him made these people so uncomfortable? Could any of these answers be based on fear, judgment and categorizing? We are all here on our own journey and are all a unique expression of God.

This man described to me how he had helped to benefit our community and I now recognize his works when I go downtown. I noticed as he spoke that others perked up to listen and maybe felt some curiosity about what he was saying. Their looks and actions seemed to move from dis-ease to ease as he spoke to me and as they watched me have a conversation with him. As I walked away from him, I had a smile in my heart as I knew he was sharing his light with me and I with him, all the while, the others had begun to take notice and listen. I take joy, solace and gratitude that I got the opportunity to meet this person who had provided improvements to our community.

I also received a quick lesson from him on judgment as I was preparing to write this chapter. He knew what the others were thinking. He saw their looks and actions. However, he somehow seemed to have no fear of others' opinions. Could it be he was comfortable with himself, that he loved himself? In fact, his first words to me were that he knew he looked funny, yet that didn't seem to bother him. He was a teacher, a professor, a dean in a university, yet now that he is retired from his physical job, he is still teaching, at least to those willing to set aside judgment, preconceived notions, and opinions, willing to listen, to learn, and to understand.

Often, we judge, we criticize, we blame, we bully, and we base our opinions on the (physical) appearance of others or on what we have learned or been told by other outside (physical) influences. This is a path of negativity that we choose to go down. Someday maybe we will choose a more loving, truthful, and accepting path that contains a willingness to learn, to listen, and to accept everyone for the unique individuals that we all are. Maybe someday we will follow our spirit, our guide, and form our own conclusions based on a particular individual's spirit, rather than their physical appearance, how they live, or what they possess. Maybe someday we will stop following the fear-based thinking, judgmental opinions of those few outside physical people and find our own truth.

We also place judgment on things. We have seen television shows of people who repair and restore dilapidated houses. At the beginning of the show, some of the homes look so run down and beyond repair that no one would even want to go around them, much less live in them. When we drive by such a house, we quickly judge it, turn away, or label it as an eyesore. However, there are those who see beyond the current physical appearance of the house and recognize the beauty it once was or could be again. They allow their positivity and creativity (skills and abilities) to work for them and continue to strengthen their skills and abilities to restore the home to its natural beauty. Maybe there's something true about the phrase *beauty lies within the eye of the beholder*.

Once the home has been restored, suddenly our opinion of it changes. We are amazed that something like that could be done. With our physical eyes, we judged the ugliness of the home, and once it's restored, we use our physical eyes to recognize the beauty of the home. When do we stop judging ourselves, other people, and things based on their current physical appearance? When do we take the time to go beyond the physical to recognize the beauty within? When do we stop judging with our physical eyes and go beyond to see real truth and beauty with our spiritual eyes?

We also judge others to take the focus off ourselves. We blame others and point fingers. We seem to be afraid (fearful) to accept responsibility for our own actions, our own lives, and possibly for our own truths. Many of us refuse to admit we may have made a mistake and are not willing to learn or to grow from it. These are our life lessons, our educational experiences. Are we willing to accept responsibility and grow, or do we remain stagnant and continue to do the same things repeatedly? When you point your finger in blame and judgment at someone else, you immediately have multiplied with your three fingers pointed back at yourself. You point the finger, and you immediately attempt to take the focus off self and place it on someone else. The day you choose to stop judging, labeling, categorizing, worrying, controlling, blaming, or demanding how you think someone else should be, or act, or live, and you begin to take responsibility for your own self, your own thoughts, and your own actions is the day your life will change and improve. It takes effort and practice, but it can be done and you can do it! You must become consciously aware of Spirit, your thoughts, and your actions, because this is what you put out into the world.

I have recognized that judgment is a choice that we make and we allow ourselves to do. When we want, envy, or worry over what others may have, how others look, or how others live their lives, then we are not accepting responsibility for our own selves, and we are judging. Every single one of us has our own journey and our own experiences, and we will receive the rewards or consequences that come with them. A few clichés to consider: People who live in glass houses should not throw stones. Walk a mile in my shoes before you judge me. Sweep off your own front porch first.

As my grandfather began to transform his way of believing, thinking, and living, he began to express that he was learning to follow *no* man. He would say, religious or not, everybody has their own opinion, but there are some who seem to base all their opinions on judgment, fear, negativity, anger, and hatred. He didn't like that approach. He didn't like being in the company of those who spoke and lived that way. He recognized and knew that was not of God. He stated that God was not about fear, hatred, and anger.

Look at what Jesus went through; he even lost his life because of fear, anger, violence, hatred, and judgment. Jesus never wavered in his faith, his teachings, his love, healing, forgiveness, and his gratitude. He listened to his Spirit, to God. He took what he had learned—truth, faith, love, wisdom, acceptance—and he taught and helped others to do the same. After being humiliated and tortured, he asked God to forgive those who had heckled, harmed, and acted in violent ways because they did not know or understand. What had Jesus done to deserve that type of treatment? Had he harmed, judged, or blamed others? How did he impact others? Didn't he teach and help others to believe and have faith in themselves, and to become the truth of who they are? Based on the negative, fear-based, judgmental opinions of a few, their fear of what they did not know or understand, their fear and negativity spread like a contagious disease, and in the end, Jesus was killed.

What are we teaching our children? Are we instilling fear, judgment, negativity, greed, control, abuse, and power? Are we pushing our children to seek and live by these types of words and actions? Are we seeing more bullying and violence in schools? Do we witness or are we the recipient of bullying from government, corporations, or people in power? Our government argues among itself, spews negativity and judgment. They spend their time blaming and pointing the finger at each other, never accepting responsibility. In the end, nothing gets accomplished, and fighting continues. Anger, judgment, fear, and violence are powerful energy forces that many of us choose to meet with counterforces, and further arguing and fighting ensue. Fear, anger, and judgment again spread like a contagious disease, and in the end, no one wins! We have proven repeatedly this does not work. Are we back to doing the same thing and expecting a different result? If we continue to choose to participate in fear, negativity, darkness, and judgment, then it will continue to grow and expand. If we choose to shine a positive light of truth, love, strength, acceptance, peace, and empowerment upon the darkness, then the darkness has no option but to dissipate in the light. When I finally was able to go within and shine the light on that dark corner in my basement, the darkness no longer had a grip on me.

When do we become accountable for our own lives, our own love, our own sense of peace, security, and well-being? When do we begin to operate from Spirit and allow it to guide us to the truth of who we are and stop following the negative opinions of a few? When do we take charge of our own lives and begin to live in a more positive, productive way and then begin to positively impact others and help others to do the same? When do we stop allowing our minds (ego, thoughts, opinions darkness, worry, and negativity) to control us or to maintain to a grip on us?

We turn on our television, and the news is riddled with violence, politics, judgment, hate, crime, drugs, abuse, and finger-pointing. Could we be absorbing this negativity into our lives and in turn modeling these behaviors for our children and those around us? What is this negativity doing to our minds (ego, thoughts)? Are we allowing negativity to become a dark blanket over our spirit? We continue to purchase and allow our children to play violent video games for hours. What could this be doing to their minds (ego and thoughts)? What could it be doing to their spirits? If we began to truly shine a light on this negativity and refused to listen to, participate in, or purchase this negative, darkness-filled stuff, then it would have no option but to dissipate and could no longer maintain a hold or a grip on us.

The Assignment

We all have our own lives and journeys and reasons why we are here. Your assignment is to recognize this for yourself and begin to find your purpose and truth. It is not in our true nature—our knowing, our spirit—to belittle, judge, harm, control, and bully another. Even though this happens on a regular basis, this is not why we are here. God is not about anger, violence, greed, control, and demands. God is about love, teaching, light, peace, wisdom, creation, and truth. We are all connected, all a part of the whole, and we are all unique with our own sets of skills and abilities. We should be allowed to grow and express ourselves in a positive, peaceful, light, loving manner. We were not placed here for judgment, bullying, anger, hatred, and violence based upon our color, race, religious beliefs, ethnicity, appearance, weight, or sexual orientation.

If you truly love and accept yourself, you will have no need to blame or judge others in an effort to take the focus off yourself. You will no longer need to seek negative attention but will be able to accept responsibility for your own life, your own thoughts, and your own actions. You will know your truth, impact others in a positive way, and allow Spirit—not your ego—to lead the way. You will teach and model this to others. What would this world be like if everyone did this?

Again, it takes a village, and it begins with you. You can model this for your family, your children, and everyone who comes along your journey.

What I have found in my journey is that there are some people in this world who seem to use their religion, the Bible, or their position of leadership or power (ego) within a company or government over others in an attempt to control others and justify their own actions and behaviors. These people are not acting from Spirit. They are acting from mind (ego). If you look at the big picture, these people are driven by outside (physical) negative influences. The vast majority of those influences usually come in the form of greed, power, jealousy, judgment, and control. Some may even use their position as an abuse of power. Instead of enhancing, developing, creating, and improving, they are causing more chaos and confusion and spreading fear in an effort to control others. They also continue to blame and point the finger, all in an effort to focus on others and take the attention and responsibility from themselves. If these people are acting this way, then they may not be operating from Spirit.

We have once again placed our beliefs in someone outside of ourselves to fix or control our lives and diminished our own truth and our own knowing. No particular man-made law or physical job or person or thing will make your life complete, peaceful, loving, accepting, and happy. If you are waiting on *someday, someone,* or *something* else to provide your happiness, your wholeness, your peace, your love, and your truth, then you will be waiting a very long time. The only way to true happiness, wholeness, and peace is to find it within and to live your own life in accordance with it.

Start believing in you—in Spirit, and begin to recognize and improve your education. Recognize that every human being, including you, is here for a purpose, a reason, and for an opportunity to learn, to experience, to teach, to grow, to love, and to be creative in establishing your own truth, establishing your own mark and your own goodness in this world.

When I worked in the psychiatric field, I used to tell my patients that God gave us two ears and one mouth so we could listen twice as much as we spoke. Try listening to Spirit (your knowing). Try listening and learning from others before speaking and judging. Begin to focus on you, focus on your Source (your knowing) and allow for the gifts you have been given. This is when several wonderful things happen:

1. Your spirit (your inherent goodness) can lead the way for you.

2. Your mind (thoughts) will begin to change and improve.
3. Your body (temple) and actions will follow.

Review your journey and your résumé. Everyone and everything you have encountered has led you to this very moment right now. What has been your educational experience? Has this chapter opened you up to a new way of looking at your life and how you teach or impact others? What are some of your life events that this chapter may have helped you to recall?

What if we as individuals reviewed our résumé, brought it into clearer focus, and began to truly enhance our lives? What if we as individuals stopped waiting on some day or others to fix, validate, and accept us? What if we as individuals began to validate ourselves, not by ego and thoughts but by Spirit? What if we as individuals stopped allowing others to take us out of our balance, our truth? What if we as individuals began to strengthen our spiritual muscles and empower ourselves with love and acceptance, and in turn, we allow that energy to flow within our own homes and out into the world?

What if everyone became aware of their true contact information, their education, work experience, references, and their unique skills and abilities? Stop waiting on convoluted, finger-pointing, judgmental laws, or others' opinions to fix your life. Get back to you—go within to Spirit. Begin to strengthen and empower yourself, your truth, your love and acceptance. Stop turning your power over to physical outside forces and influences such news, politicians, and corporations.

As my grandfather told me, "Follow no man." He stated, "You need to follow your spirit, for it will never steer you wrong." He also would smile and say, "You can't go wrong if you always go right!" As I've come to remember that statement during my journey, I now know he was so very right. Some people may have more education, some people may have more common sense, but those are skills and abilities. Everyone has something positive and creative they are good at. The question is, have they recognized it and what are they doing with it? Are they enhancing their skills and abilities for the good of others and impacting others in a positive light, or are they using them to control, manipulate, and place blame in an effort to take the focus off of themselves?

I close this chapter with yet more questions:

- What if we began to love and accept ourselves?
- What if we let go of outside negative forces, took responsibility for our own lives and how we live, and discovered our own truths of who we are?
- What if we stopped allowing others to tell us who we are and what we need to be doing?

In turn, we could start a ripple effect or a movement of positive ways of being and allow that energy to flow through us and to those around us. What would your life be like if you did this? What would the world around you be like if we all began to do this?

SELF-REFLECTION

(This space is provided for you to reflect on
how you can apply what you've read.)

CHAPTER 13

Forgiveness and Gratitude

FORGIVENESS AND GRATITUDE ARE PROBABLY the greatest keys to unlocking the chains that bind you and for opening doors in your life. We've all experienced events in which we've felt hurt or wronged by someone else, whether the act was intentional or unintentional. We've also played a role in hurting or wronging someone else in our lives, whether the act was intentional or unintentional. No matter what the event was, it was by a choice either the other person or you made. Some of these choices may have caused pain, anger, or hurt that led to you leaving someone or being left by someone. Some choices may have been very painful for you or caused extreme pain to someone else. Some or our choices may have led to an extreme that caused bodily harm or even death. For your résumé, this corresponds to your educational experience. What have you learned and what are you learning?

For example, making a choice to drink and drive and causing a wreck in which someone was badly injured or even killed. It was a choice to drink, and it was a choice to drive. Whether you believe it was an intentional act or not, it still caused pain and suffering. Another example might be that we may find we are in love with another person and choose to leave our current relationship for someone else. Whether you believe it is an intentional act or not, it still causes pain and suffering.

If you made the choice that caused pain and suffering to someone else, you must learn to forgive. If you are the person that has been the recipient of pain and suffering, you too must learn to forgive. How? You have to go within and forgive yourself for the pain and suffering you have caused and begin to make better choices for yourself. You will need to learn what is causing you to make these kinds of choices that cause pain and suffering to others. You also must gain an awareness of how you are hurting yourself. If you do not find forgiveness, strength, peace, love (spirit, truth, knowing) within yourself and begin to redefine your thoughts and your actions, then you are on a road to repeating the same patterns. These patterns will continue to manifest or mirror into more hurt, pain, and suffering not only for you but also for those around you.

If you have been hurt or wronged by someone, you still need to go within and find forgiveness for yourself and for the person you feel hurt you. You must begin to realize the strength and love for the person you truly are. If you continue to hold on to the hurt and pain and feel animosity toward the person who hurt you, you will keep yourself bound in chains of pain, anger, hate, and despair. If you carry that anger, blame, hurt, and pain within, then it will continue to burden you, to hold you, and to fester within you. If this is what you continue to choose to carry within you, then it will be what you put out into the world and will return or be mirrored back to you. You will remain in the constant cycle of pain and find yourself in other painful situations until you choose to free yourself from it.

Our life is a journey, a school of life. Everyone we meet has a purpose and a role in our classroom. We too have a role or purpose in this classroom. Some people will test us, some will love us, some will leave us; some we will leave, some will teach us, and some may learn from us. It is our choice as to how we deal with others while we are in class. It is our choice how we respond to or how we treat others while we are in class. It is our choice whether we learn from these experiences, pass our lessons, graduate, and move forward. Otherwise, we end up repeating the lessons until we learn them. When we feel wronged or hurt, a significant part of our education is to find and allow for forgiveness. Otherwise, we will continue to carry that pain, anger, and hurt within us and likely repeat the same cycles and lessons.

Oftentimes when we feel pain and refuse to forgive, we end up punishing ourselves. We may become obsessed with negative thinking, blame, revenge, or obsessive or acting-out behaviors. We may throw ourselves into work or extreme exercise. We may use alcohol or drugs. We fall into our coping mechanisms. All this thinking and behavior will provide is a mask to cover up the real issue. It will not allow you to deal effectively with the fear, pain, hurt, or anger. This renders us incapable of effective healing, growth, and the ability to move forward in life.

Forgiveness is not an act of weakness but rather an act of strength.

True forgiveness can unlock your chains of despair and free you from carrying that burden. Forgiveness is for you and will be the key to setting you free. Take a moment and identify someone you need to forgive. How will you forgive that person and release the chains that bind you? It does not mean the other person will get away with the choice they made to harm you. It means that you no longer choose to give your power, your energy, and your strength to them. It means you *choose* to let go and no longer continue to carry that negativity, fear, and pain. It means you will no longer carry those burdens. When you go within to Spirit, there is no fear, no hate, no anger, no guilt, and no pain. These negative, fear-based thoughts are only found within the mind, which will continue to lead you into further obsessive thinking and behaviors—if you choose to allow it.

With the act of forgiveness, you also need to forgive yourself for being angry, hurtful, or in pain. Forgiveness is choosing not to beat yourself up or to blame yourself for something you should have or could have done differently. Do not fall into the "what's wrong with me" or "what did I do" attention-seeking mentality. You cannot change the past; you can only learn from it. Forgiveness is also choosing to release the hatred, guilt, or anger toward the person you felt harmed you.

Forgiveness is a choice that only you can make, but it will provide you with the freedom and strength to move forward in your life. Forgiveness unlocks your chains. Gratitude opens your doors.

Gratitude is a gift that you need to incorporate in your daily life. Learn to be grateful for your health, your family, your job, and your home. Learn to be grateful for all that you are. Gratitude is important to be consciously aware of on a daily basis, just like the acts of kindness and of giving and receiving. Being grateful is an action; it is something you *do*. The act of being grateful is a way to raise your vibrational energy level to a higher realm and a higher way of being. When you are truly grateful, you *feel* it and you *know* it in your heart, in your spirit. It is a feeling or a sense of a higher, peaceful joy and love. As long as you practice gratitude, you are opening your doors, and you will always receive more to appreciate. For with gratitude, there is no room for negativity and doubt. Are you exhibiting gratitude each day? Do you recognize and express it each day? Identify at least three things you are grateful for; you can use the space provided at the end of this chapter.

I've come to incorporate gratitude when I awaken, throughout my day, and each night before I go to bed. *I am* grateful for all the things that happened to me during that day, and I give thanks for all that I received or accomplished. I know each night that I still have more to do, but I am grateful for all that I have done and recognize the gifts I received throughout my day. Whether I began a task, completed a task, made someone smile or laugh, or provided someone with an opportunity to share with me—I am grateful that I made it through the day and did the best I could to accomplish or work through the events that crossed my path.

Some encounters may have come in the form of acts of kindness or sowing a seed. Some encounters may have come in the form of lessons or tests designed to pull me out of my balance. Some encounters may attempt to disrupt my energy and my flow. I know when those negative or disruptive events show up in my day, I must recognize how they affect my energy and realize this is education and it's my choice as to how I respond. We all have choices when negativity arises. It is our choice to counter with negativity or work to remain in our balance and resolve the matter positively, peacefully, and effectively. It is our choice to forgive or to burden ourselves further. When I feel I have been able to remain in my balance and work through a crisis, I am grateful because I know I did the best I could, and the outcome of the situation is usually resolved effectively.

I take time in my day and in the evening to process and to learn from the events or lessons of the day and to be grateful for them all. When you start being more consciously aware of what you do, how you act, how you respond, and what you put out into the world, then you will begin the process of being grateful for it, and in turn more wonderful gifts will come. This is truth. This is strength. This is empowerment. This is enlightenment. I've learned it, and I've experienced it. It has now become a way of life for me. Be loving, kind, and consciously aware of what you think and what you say and do throughout your day. Be consciously aware of how you treat yourself and how you treat others. You should always take time to be grateful for who you are, for your gifts, and what you have encountered in your day. As you do this, you strengthen your spiritual muscle, you raise your energy, and you become stronger, more empowered, and enlightened. As you grow, it will grow and begin to manifest and multiply.

- What burdens are you carrying?
- What chains do you need to unlock and release?
- Who will you forgive today?
- What will you be grateful for today?
- What doors and dreams would you like to open?
- When crises or lessons come, how will you respond?

SELF-REFLECTION

(This space is provided for you to reflect on
how you can apply what you've read.)

CHAPTER 14

The Resume of Life

THROUGHOUT THIS BOOK, I'VE TOUCHED on key terms and words, and I have used them interchangeably. These words express feelings of positive, conscious awareness, creativity, and growth.

These positive words have become affirmations that I use in my daily life. I have come to believe in these words and use them to become who *I am*.

As I stated in the beginning, I have been hurt and judged and experienced pain, worry, fear, struggle, rejection, and loss. Also, I expressed that you may not know me in the physical sense, but you do know me in the spiritual realm, as we are all connected and all a part of a whole.

My journey is not the same as yours, for we all experience different events in our lives, and we all have our own journeys to walk. However, we all have feelings, and we all encounter events in our lives that lead to various feelings of joy, abundance, love, faith, peace, beauty, and trust. We also encounter events that lead to feelings of hurt, fear, grief, struggle, judgment, blame, worry, and pain. No one can measure if one person's pain is greater than someone else's. Conversely, no one can measure if one person's joy is greater than someone else's. The fact is it is our own joy or our own pain that we experience. The depth to which it is felt can only be measured by the person experiencing it. We are also the one to find our balance, love, acceptance, enlightenment, and peace.

In the big scheme of things, there are actually two things in this world that we need to be absolutely clear on. Those two things are love and fear. Love comes from within, from Spirit, God, your knowing, your truth. Fear comes from your mind, your thoughts, your ego, and has been placed there by external physical entities. Fear causes worry, anxiety, pain, and judgment. What purpose is any of this providing for you? Does it keep you bound in chains or cause your coping mechanisms to kick in? Does fear affect your overall health, attitude, and well-being? Do you allow fear to affect you in a negative way, and also cause you to impact others negatively?

We can choose to live our lives in love and experience peace, light, joy, strength, abundance, enlightenment, and truth. We can also choose to live our lives in fear and continue to remain in struggle, pain, anger, worry, and negativity. This is your free will and your choice. Here are some examples of fear for you to review and think about:

- dying
- loss
- pain
- illness
- love and intimacy
- fear of being alone
- being happy
- being hurt (physically and/or emotionally)
- being rejected
- fear of labels
- fear of losing
- fear of winning
- fear of letting go
- fear of success
- fear of being who we truly are
- fear of what others might think
- fear of not measuring up or being good enough
- fear of not having enough

After reading this list, ask yourself, "What am I afraid of and how have I allowed this fear to impact my life?"

Living with Fear

You know, we are just plain afraid of living! We are afraid that if we found our truth and our purpose and became who we truly are, then others may judge us and reject us, or we might not measure up. Some of us are even fearful of being wrong. In essence, by *thinking* this way, we are judging ourselves! None of these examples are based on love, Spirit, and the truth of who we are within. We are relying on outside influences, opinions, and even our own negative thoughts to keep us bound in our chains and stunt our growth. This reminds me of a profound statement from President Franklin D. Roosevelt: "The only thing we have to fear is fear itself." For some reason, many of us seem to be unwilling to go within to find our true selves, our true love. We seem to be unwilling to accept that we are here for a purpose. We are afraid to let our light shine!

We can continue to sweep things under our rug of fear and make excuses for others and ourselves; however, eventually one of two things will happen: the pile will get so large we will trip and fall over it, or it becomes a mountain that we cannot climb.

If you have ever flown on a rainy, cloudy day, once the plane takes off and soars through the clouds, you find the sky is actually peaceful, beautiful, and blue. You also notice the clouds are beneath you. This is energy because everything is always flowing and moving. I use this analogy because we all experience rainy, cloudy times in our lives. However, do we realize that if we allow ourselves to increase our energy in a positive way, that we too can soar through those clouds and will find peaceful, beautiful blue skies?

As I have begun to transition to love, to Spirit, and to negate my fears, I have begun to fill my life with peace, abundance, balance, gratitude, enlightenment, and joy. My physical job performance has improved; I get more done in less time and with less struggle. I no longer turn my power and my energy over to people or forces beyond my control. I have learned to keep a check on my energy and to remain in my balance and truth. I have learned that if I allow outside negative influences to remove me from my balance and I begin to react with a negative counterforce based on fear and anger, it never resolves anything. In fact, it only causes more struggle, worry, and anxiety. This frustration affects my mental, emotional, and physical well-being.

By continuing to work on me and remain in balance, my relationships have improved, and I find joy in doing things again. I have begun to expand upon my creativity and have more energy, more joy, abundance, gratitude, and balance in my life. I have also recognized that I enjoy being around and helping others again. I have found that others seem to enjoy my presence as well. I am not the same sad, hurt, miserable, weak, worried, fearful person I was a few years ago. I no longer expend my energy running and seeking other people and things to provide my happiness. I am stronger. I am more loving, kind, abundant, and peaceful than I have ever been, and I found it all through Spirit. Spirit was within me all along, simply waiting for me to recognize it, accept it, strengthen it, and grow with it. We *all* have it within us; we just need to recognize, accept, grow, and strengthen it.

Have you ever thought or said, "If I knew then what I know now," or, "If I could go back and change it I would"? The fact is our lives are our journeys, and we are here to learn, to experience, to help, to teach, and to grow. These experiences are what build our résumé. We are here to love and to accept ourselves and to grow and to see the good in ourselves and to recognize the good in others (namaste). We must find our goodness, our peace, our love, our beauty, and our light and share that in the world that we create from Spirit. We can't go back and change our past, but we can learn from it, improve upon our lives today, and carry it forward on our journeys. We can forgive ourselves for the pain or hurt we have caused others. We can forgive others for the pain and hurt they may have caused us. We can allow everyone to live their lives and to experience their lives (their journey) in love, in acceptance, in peace, and in truth. We can perform acts of kindness to everyone we encounter on our journeys, and we can sow positive seeds of love, light, joy, and acceptance. We can begin to take care of self and in turn become stronger and more enlightened to help others. All of this comes from Spirit, not from external physical forces.

The popular band Sugarland may have said it best (my paraphrased version) in their song, "Something More": "Some believe in destiny, and some believe in fate, I believe that happiness is something we create."

The best news of all is that we can learn from our past (résumé) and obtain a better awareness of how we arrived to the place we are today. We can gain an awareness of where we want to go on our journeys and recognize the positive impact we can provide. We can begin to do it right now. Recognize your beauty and your energy. Recognize the beauty and the energy in your spiritual mirror and become more consciously aware of the beauty and energy that surround you through nature and within others. Learn from your past, observe and take notice of your present, and if you want to change things, then make the effort and the choice to do so. It begins with you! It begins with Spirit! Keep in mind that everything and everyone you have experienced in your résumé has led you to here and now. What you choose to learn and take from those experiences is up to you.

We must understand that everything happens at the right time and for the right reason. If God brings you to it, God will bring you through it. God (Spirit) is in all things, and as we all know, life happens! Isn't that why we are here—to experience, to learn, to grow, and to help? It is time we get out of our own way (thoughts, mind, worry, ego) and stop worrying about what others think. It's time we stop worrying about what others think we should be doing or what we think others should be doing. It is time to deal with self—with Spirit. In the drug and alcohol treatment world, we referred to those fear-based, worrisome, negative thoughts as stinkin' thinkin'.

We must go within to find our own true purpose, recognize our strength and our own potential. This is our purpose and why we are here. Events along our journeys come as lessons, experiences, and gifts. Some experiences may be painful and may come in the form of a loss. Sometimes you may feel like you will never catch a break or that the "hits" just keep coming. This is when you must understand what you are supposed to be learning from these events and hold on to your faith more than ever. Sometimes we may feel that nothing is happening for us, but I can assure you that is never the case. *Something* is always happening, whether we recognize it at the time or not. That is the energy we are made up of and are surrounded by. As you now know, energy is always flowing and moving.

God (Spirit) is in all things, but do we really recognize this? If it is supposed to be, then it will be. There is much wisdom in the cliché "Let go and let God!" If it is not right, then stop trying to control and manipulate a situation to be a certain way based with your thoughts. Allow yourself to be open and peaceful. Then allow for it to transpire and unfold just how it should. This is truly a practice in faith. This is where you put Spirit first and refuse to operate solely from your mind and your wants. Otherwise, you are back to trying to fit a square peg in a round hole. As I explained earlier, you end up expending worrisome, frustrating energy trying to change, grasp, or control something or someone that eventually will be lost or destroyed. During the time you are expending all the energy to force or control something or someone, you must understand that it will never bring you true, lasting happiness and peace. Some things you have to let go of and stop trying to hold or grasp or control. Otherwise, you will remain in a constant state of struggle and expend a lot of energy on something that you want that may not actually be what you need for your journey. I remind you of the poem, "Woman with Flower."

There may be times we need to rest, to listen, to refuel, and to continue to be faithful. Geoffrey Chaucer was right when he wrote years ago, "Patience is a virtue." However, patience has been one of the most difficult lessons for me, even to this day. At least I am now consciously aware of this and continue to work and strengthen it.

Sometimes events come as miraculous, joyful, exciting gifts or opportunities. This is truly a time to be grateful. Sometimes we receive tests and even some pop quizzes. In both cases, it is our responsibility to find what we are to learn by these events, to take care of ourselves, and to be grateful for all that we have been given. What doesn't kill you makes you stronger.

As I have come to the end of this book, I would be remiss in not mentioning that day when I told a friend on the phone about meeting my trainer. I stated that I didn't know where this was going, but I was surrendering to it. Somehow, I guess I knew that God had brought this person to me at the right time for the right reason. At the time, I only looked at it as losing some weight; however, as I opened up and allowed for help, it became so much more. She became a confidante, a friend, and helped me to rebuild my strength and my confidence. She did not judge me for my looks, my weight, or my past. On the contrary, she supported and helped me to become more aware of my energy, my strength, my health, my nutrition, and she helped me to begin to grow and to learn. She was able to teach me because I was finally ready and willing to listen, to accept, to allow for help, and to learn.

I always knew I had a book inside of me but never knew what to do with it, what it would be about. Nor did I have the strength and willpower (energy) to begin it, much less to complete it. It has been over two years since I met my trainer and began the journey of rebuilding my physical self. It has been over a year since I met my spiritual adviser. Once again, when I was ready and willing to surrender, to learn, and to allow for help, God brought another person into my life when I needed it, at the right time for the right reason. This time I was opening up and paying attention to the signs along my journey. I needed to be humbled, to surrender, to listen, to pay attention, to accept and allow for help. I was ready and willing to allow for help and finally begin to believe and focus on my spiritual self. She helped me to open up and to understand about Spirit so that I could stop running, worrying, and hiding, and finally start *believing.*

Everything I have experienced, everything I have done, everyone I have encountered in my life has led me to here and now. I now know that *I am* on the right path and am no longer on a path of self-defeating, self-destructive fear and worry. I no longer worry about those who may or may not love and accept me. I no longer try to control or fix events or others. I no longer worry about where I fit in, because I know and believe that I am a unique expression of God, of Spirit. So are *you!* Believe me when I say that knowing and believing this truth removes a great deal of effort, struggle, worry, and work.

You may recall that my spiritual adviser told me that my grandfather had left me something and wanted to know if I had received it. After studying, committing, writing, and finishing this book, the answer is a resounding yes! I have received *it!* Thank you, Pappaw! You left me *spiritual truth* and *awareness* and set me on the path to *spiritual consciousness!* I am here; I am no longer running in fear or pain. I am strong. I am love, *I am faith believin'*, and now I have come full circle from where you began to teach me! Spirit, mind, and body have come together as a whole, and I can now share it with others just as you did with me.

Shortly after I came to recognize what my grandfather had left me, I was speaking with some family members and telling them about his Bible and teachings. They looked at me with astonishment and stated, "Terry, we have that Bible," and asked if I would like to have it. Tears filled my eyes, as I had thought his Bible had long been discarded, and now it was coming home with me. It was then that I truly realized the time had come for me to receive all that he had left for me, and what a gift it was. When I got it home, there were some of his writings still within it, and everything that I had already written in this book was on point with all he had taught me so many years ago.

I am so grateful for the peace, love, light, joy, awareness, freedom, and abundance I have obtained in my life. I am grateful for all the events and people I have encountered along my journey, as they helped me to get to where I am today. Whether I was accepted or rejected, whether the events were joyful or painful, they were all a part of my journey in an effort for me to learn, to teach, to wake up, and to grow. I just had to figure that out, and now I am sharing it with you.

Most of us have lived our lives with the simple phrase of mind, body, and spirit. However, if you believe teachings from the Bible, God said, "Do not put others before me." In essence, don't we put mind and body before Spirit even by just saying this simple phrase?

In times of crisis, we seem to pick up Spirit, pray, and even beg for help. Once the crisis is over, we tend to push our snooze button, set Spirit aside, and go back to sleep. We put Spirit back down and move on with our mind (our thoughts, our ego), and our body (our actions) obviously follows. We go back to the thinking and searching for outside people and things, or we allow negativity to reinforce our mind. We do this all in an effort to make something work or to make us happy.

What if we stopped pushing our snooze button once the crisis is over and kept Spirit first in our lives always? What if we always put Spirit first whether there is a crisis or not? What if we allowed Spirit to feed and to lead our mind, and then our body would follow? In the paraphrased lyrics of the popular band Fleetwood Mac—"You can go your own way. You can open up as everything is waiting for you, or you can call it another lonely day."

Your Choice, Your Free Will

We all have something that we are passionate about. We all have something that brings us true joy and a sense of peace and happiness. We all have something inside of us just waiting to come out, to create and to expand upon. Remove the physical environment, the noise, the chaos, and any possible financial gain you think it may provide you and go within to find it and cocreate with it and to expand your true self.

If you love landscaping, then do it. If you love helping others, then do it. If you love helping animals, then do it. If you love organizing, cleaning, or decorating, then do it. If you love writing, drawing, singing, dancing, or painting, then do it. If you are mechanically or electronically inclined, then do it. Whatever you love to do and whatever brings out your passion, your joy, and your peace from within, then this is what you need to do. Expand upon it and find a way to incorporate it and strengthen it on a regular basis in your life. This is your cocreation with Spirit and will enhance and beautify your world and the world around you. These are your unique skills and abilities. This is who you are and will help to build your spiritual muscle and to grow. God, Spirit, Source is about love, creation, believing, and growing into all you can be. It wants you to live and experience a wonderful, joyful, and fulfilled life. God, Spirit, Source wants you to love and accept yourself and to begin to mirror that out into your world. God, Spirit, Source is not about fear, anger, pain, worry, opinions, greed, control, violence, and struggle.

Your résumé of life is not the same as mine, but the experiences and feelings you have encountered are similar. Your journey has brought about feelings of love, light, joy, abundance, and peace, and it has also brought feelings of fear, pain, grief, struggle, worry, judgment, and loss. It has also brought questions and a feeling of faith. I pray this book has brought enlightenment to you and you've become more consciously aware of your Spirit (truth, love, creativity, strength, peace) and how your mind (thoughts, ego, fear, judgment, worry, blame, control) and body (temple health, actions) have impacted your life and the lives of those around you.

I have provided various examples in my résumé of what I have learned, experienced, lost, and obtained. I have given specific examples of God-Spirit providing me with people and events right on time and for the right reasons. As I have continued to trust in the process, kept my *faith believin'*, and moved forward in doing my part to believe, to strengthen, to listen, to learn, and even to finish the book, I have also recognized and allowed for others to enter my journey, be it old friends or new acquaintances. I have allowed myself to be open and not to close myself off in judgment or fear. As with the gentleman I met at the doctor's office, he came and offered me just what I needed, right on time and for the right reasons—all in an effort to help me write the "Judgment" chapter.

I have come to realize that if you judge or live in fear, you close yourself off to new opportunities, to new possibilities, and to learn from others. Everyone has offered their unique skills and abilities in an effort to help and support me on this endeavor.

I refer to these opening doors as miracles. I have become more consciously aware of miracles and try to recognize them each day as I continue on my journey. Some miracles may be huge and easy to recognize, and some may seem small, but they are all miracles, and I am grateful for them. By being consciously aware and grateful, those doors opened *right on time* and for the *right reasons*. You see, we truly are connected! We must believe and continue to do our part. Then everything we need will be provided for us right on time and for the right reasons.

Whether events or people were provided as a lesson, a pop quiz, or a wonderful gift, it was ultimately my choice to either push my snooze button or to wake up and recognize it as such. Everything and everyone on my journey came so that I could learn, listen, grow, teach, and give and receive love, acceptance, and gratitude. I just had to finally realize and become consciously aware of the events, people, and places that I have encountered and to know it's all been specific and relevant to my journey. Whether I understood it at the time, found a way to understand it later, or maybe never completely understood it, it was all there to help me to recognize and to become more of who I am meant to be.

Establishing Your Resume of Life

You are the one to find your own answers if you are ready to ask the questions. Just like doing your job résumé, you have to acknowledge, review, and provide the criteria to create a great life résumé. Your contact information, your objective, your education, your work experience, your skills and abilities, and your references when put together as a whole demonstrate your potential.

Take the time to see what you have done to meet the requirements for the life job for which you are applying. Your life events, passion, journey, experiences, and references are the basis for your résumé of life. Instead of leaving the pieces of your puzzle scattered all around, recognize and understand how to put the pieces of the puzzle together. By doing this, you are becoming whole. If you only operate by mind and body, you are leaving out Spirit. In the physical sense, you are like a car trying to drive down the road with only three tires. As you see, everything must work together to function properly and to function as a whole. I pray this book has inspired and motivated you to do just that.

Have you reviewed your experiences and realized how the events led you to where you are now? Are you happy where you are now? What are you passionate about? What experiences are virtually similar and led to the same or similar outcomes? What might you need to do to stop falling in the same patterns and receiving the same outcomes? The answers to these questions and more will come from your Source of Being.

If we do not learn our lessons, we are destined to repeat them in different ways until we do figure them out. History does have a tendency to repeat itself, wouldn't you say? You are the only one who can choose to remain in the same cycle or to learn and to change the cycle.

You are the only one who can take the steps to improve your life or to remain where you are. You are the only one who can look to your Source and find your mirror and to establish your *faith believin'* within yourself. You are the only one to go within, ask the questions, and listen for the answers. You are the only one who can forgive yourself and others, or you can continue to hold on to the fear, blame, worry, judgment, grief, and anger. You are the only one who can go within and choose to communicate with your Source of Being. You are the only one who can choose to nurture yourself and begin to grow, to create, and to expand your energy. Otherwise, you can choose to remain in the binding chains of pain, stagnation, fear, judgment, worry, anger and struggle. The only person standing in your way of your truth and your purpose is you. The only person who can change your ways of being, thinking, and doing is you.

It's your time, and you have now to do it. It costs nothing, and you have been given free will (choice) to do it. The questions are: Are you ready? And will you make that choice?

SELF-REFLECTION

(This space is provided for you to reflect on
how you can apply what you've read.)

CONSCIOUSLY AWARE

My dear friend,

After *The Résumé of Life* was completed, I took some time off to reflect over the past year and wanted to share an update and reflection with you.

As I sit here at the end of the first day of vacation and reflect over the past year, it's been amazing! I completed my book *The Résumé of Life*. I am now working on two more books! I began my company, Inspire and Motivate (IAM), and am continuing to awaken in an effort to help others.

I've had the opportunity to rekindle old friendships and even make new friends via the books and through the power of social media. Everyone comes into our lives at the right time and for the right reasons. It's our choice to recognize this or not.

As I watch the sun set over the ocean, I am astounded by the magnitude of energy and peace that it provides. My heart is filled with love, peace, and acceptance as I know that I too am made up of this energy—we all are! We are all connected, all a part of the whole, and if we will just allow ourselves to recognize this, our potential is unlimited.

Just as there is a law of gravity, there is also a law of attraction. What you feel on the inside and what you put out into the world is what you will receive or what will be reflected back to you. If you have a heart filled with love, positivity, and peace, then that is what will reflect back to you. If you are filled with worry, stress, negativity, and chaos, then you will continue to receive more of the same. It's your choice to become more consciously aware of your feelings, your thoughts, your surroundings, and your actions. As I said earlier, life is a journey, a school of life, and we are here to teach, to learn, and to make this world a better place.

As I have continued to progress on my journey, to focus on being more consciously aware, and to believe in me and the power of Spirit, I have found that my life is becoming more peaceful and fulfilled.

Many of us are caught up in a corporate world, and we allow those constant demands to chisel away at our hearts, our minds, and even our physical health. When you back away and look at the big picture, such as the ocean, the sun, the stars, the true energy, and the beauty that surrounds us, those worldly things or problems begin to take on a new and lesser meaning.

My journey of love and light has just begun over the past few years, and now I believe there is more to do, more to teach, and more to learn, but at least as I write this today and share it with you, I *know* I'm on the right path. My heart is filled with so much gratitude, and *I am* so very grateful for the beautiful, inspiring, heartfelt messages from readers.

As I stated in the beginning of the book, everyone and everything has led me to here and now. It is the same for you. We are here to experience our lessons, learn from them, and find a way to put the pieces of our puzzle together in an effort to learn, to grow, to love, and to accept ourselves and others for the truth of who we are: (I am). Once I stopped running and began to take a real look at my life, began to understand my spiritual mirror and to accept accountability for who *I am*, this is when my life truly began to change and improve.

I've outlined my steps and shared my journey with you in hopes that you will find solace, peace, balance, love, and acceptance for yourself and become consciously aware of where you have been, where you are now, and where you wish to go.

So I take this opportunity to express my gratitude, my love, my light, and my acceptance to you. I wish you love and light on your journey—your résumé—your school of life.

Namaste.

ABOUT THE AUTHOR

TERRY BEGAN HER CAREER WORKING as a probation officer for adolescents in the community. She provided intensive probation and individual and family counseling. She also helped to develop a program for children and teens in the community in an effort to give kids alternatives to getting into trouble.

She has worked as a therapist for children and families for more than fifteen years and helped to develop alcohol and drug-abuse awareness programs for children and teens. She was a program director for a dual-diagnosis residential treatment center for adolescents where she developed therapeutic programs and provided individual, group, and family therapy.

Over the past fourteen years, she has also worked in the medical sales and customer-service industry, where she also provided motivational sales and customer-service training techniques to colleagues and clients.

Terry is a passionate advocate for living one's truth. During her journey, like you, she has encountered numerous successes and pitfalls and has taken the time to try to figure it out. Her life's goal is to inspire and motivate others to live their truth.

Terry holds a master of arts degree in educational psychology and counseling from Tennessee Tech University and a bachelor of science degree in mass communications from Middle Tennessee State University.

A business owner (Inspire and Motivate, IAM, LLC) and motivational speaker, Terry is the author of three books: *Bridging the Gap: An Educator's Guide*, *Bridging the Gap: A Parent's Guide*, and *The Résumé of Life: Becoming Consciously Aware Through Spirit, Mind, and Body*.

To invite Terry to inspire and motivate your group at your next event, you may contact her at terry@iamterryjwalker.com or visit her website: IAMTerryJWalker.com.

Printed in the United States
By Bookmasters